My PINEAPPLES *Went to* HOUSTON

Finding the Humor in My Dashed Hopes,
Broken Dreams and Plans Gone Outrageously Awry

Dear Jennifer,

Thank you so much
for helping me.
celebrate my pineapples!
Enjoy the book —
Lee

LEE GAITAN

outskirtspress
DENVER, COLORADO

Outskirts Press, Inc.
http://www.outskirtspress.com

ISBN: 978-1-4787-2351-6

Outskirts Press and the "OP" logo are trademarks belonging to Outskirts Press, Inc.

PRINTED IN THE UNITED STATES OF AMERICA

Contents

Introduction

LATE IN THE last century, 1998 of the Common Era to be a little more precise, I was seated next to a delightful older gentleman on an early morning flight from Miami to Atlanta. As we chatted, I explained that I was returning home from a short publicity tour to promote the release of my first book, *Falling Flesh Just Ahead*, a collection of humorous essays about women in midlife.

"A publicity tour! Well, that sounds downright glamorous," he declared. "How did everything go?"

"Uh," I hesitated, "not nearly as glamorously as I had envisioned." We both laughed as I recounted to my seatmate the many well-laid plans that had gone everywhere from a little bit to a whole lot awry.

"Nothing, but nothing, in my life ever seems to go quite way it is supposed to," I concluded.

He chuckled and nodded in understanding. He then began relating his own tale of woe. He explained that he was on his way back from a month-long stay in Guatemala, where he and his wife had gone to help with relief efforts following the devastation of a hurricane. No one had asked them to go, nor were they being paid for their time or expenses; they were retired, had the time and means to do it and simply felt compelled to follow their hearts. He quickly shrugged off my attempts to commend them. He and his wife couldn't accept any thanks or recognition for simply doing what they felt was the right thing to do, he said with true modesty.

"The only thing we really did want," he added, almost a bit embarrassed, "was a crate of fresh pineapples. The pineapples in Guatemala are out of this world. Nothing like what you get in the grocery stores here," he said.

To that end, he had bought a crate of pineapples and made arrangements with the airline for them to be shipped home as a surprise for his wife. A great plan, but life being life, the plan had developed a few hitches along the way. Due to inclement weather and the airline industry's notorious expertise at screwing up every travel plan, the simple goal of getting himself, his wife and his pineapples home to Missouri had become a logistical nightmare. By the time he sat down next to me on this flight to Atlanta, he had been awake for 28 hours, had been routed and re-routed to two different airports and had been bumped off three planes, sending him, his wife and their baggage to three separate destinations.

"S-o-o-o," he drawled, "right now I'm going to Atlanta to catch another flight to St. Louis, my wife's waiting for a direct flight back in Miami, and my pineapples…well, my pineapples went to Houston."

"That's brilliant!" I exclaimed to my seatmate. "That's the truth for all of us at some time or other."

He agreed, and as we laughed again, I thought of all the plans we make, all the ways we try to control every situation in our lives. We try so hard to dot every "i" and cross every "t," but sometimes, despite our best efforts, our pineapples go to Houston anyway. And there's not one thing we can do about it, except decide how we will respond. Will it be with humor and acceptance or with anger and resistance? The man sitting next to me then had clearly made his choice. By all accounts, he should have been annoyed at best and out-and-out livid at worst, but he was instead calm and pleasant and actually making light of his ordeal.

"I'm telling you right now," I said laughing, but not joking, "I am stealing your pineapples line for the title of my next book."

I'd already begun making notes of all the crazy "pineapple"

moments that I'd had just since starting the book tour. Being featured on a radio show with a guy billed as "the thinking man's redneck" was certainly near the top of the list. Heaven knows, I thought, modern life is rife with opportunities for our pineapples to be misdirected on an hourly basis. You mistakenly grab a pack of gum instead of your flash drive and are left to make an important presentation with only your minty fresh breath to back you up. Your cell phone cuts out for three seconds and a heartfelt apology dissipates into thin air, taking an important relationship with it. You change one teensy little vowel and suddenly instead of asking a hotel clerk in Italy for your room key, you are asking him in very explicit terms to have sex with you... right now...because you really need it...*per favore, signore*. Okay, maybe that last one only happened to me, but still, I thought, a light-hearted book about plans gone outrageously awry would surely have universal appeal. And if it produced enough laughs to defuse one or two cases of road rage, well, that would be gravy. Low fat gravy, of course.

But a funny thing happened on the way to publishing that next book. A little something I refer to as "shock and awfulness," otherwise known as 2002, the year that signaled the beginning of the end of life as I knew it. The second year of the 21st century kicked off with my father's death, went on to see my mother hover for days on the edge of a coma and finished big with—the cherry on top—my husband of 22 years secretly losing all of our money on a hare-brained business venture and running off to Arizona to live with an ex-stripper and her five children. And it was all downhill from there! The events of 2002 ushered in a series of calamities that reduced nearly everything I held dear to rubble and set me reeling for the next decade.

To clarify, it wasn't really my father's death or my mother's illness that set the destruction in motion. Losing my dad and seeing my mom critically ill were not easy or pleasant experiences, but neither were they wholly unanticipated. The exact timing caught me by surprise, but I obviously knew my parents were aging and had begun to brace myself a bit for the inevitable. Still, while those events did not destroy me, they did leave me shaken and feeling vulnerable—and definitely not in the best shape to sustain a catastrophic blow. That catastrophic blow, the one that set the violent destruction in motion, came shortly thereafter when my husband, the man with whom I'd shared my heart and life for more than two decades, glanced across the living room at me and unceremoniously stated, "I'm leaving."

That was it. That was all he said. Just "I'm leaving." For him, a simple two-word declaration. For me, a two-word Molotov cocktail tossed into the dead center of my life. Tossed without emotion. Without explanation. Without warning. The proverbial preemptive strike, the one I never saw coming. I had no time to steady myself against its force. No time to cover my head or shield my eyes. No time to grab for precious mementos or take one last look around the place. Just "I'm leaving" and then…boom! A colossal boom. A blinding, deafening, raging boom. A cataclysmic boom that blasted all 23 years of our life together into a zillion broken pieces.

From overwhelming shock and unbearable grief to emotional numbness and total paralysis, I seemed to cycle through every stage on a daily basis. And no part of it struck me as particularly humorous. In the aftermath of the explosion, writing a lighthearted book about life's wacky "pineapple" moments was both far from my mind and far out of my skill set. It was all I could do to stand upright. I didn't think I would ever see life as wacky again. In fact, my life seemed to become more about constant whacks than wackiness. Every time I tried to pull myself up and put one foot in front of the other—whack!—I was knocked over again by one of the countless repercussions set off by those two little words, "I'm leaving." There was not one aspect of my life, from my finances to my family to my mental and physical health that wasn't seriously bruised or battered.

Then one day in the midst of all the chaos—somewhere between loud cursing and crying, I believe—the pineapples metaphor came back to me, and I had to laugh, almost perversely, but laugh nonetheless, at how far past Houston my pineapples had gone. They were surely as far south as Tierra del Fuego, I surmised, and likely heading up the other side of the globe. Talk about plans gone outrageously awry! In that small moment of laughter, I suddenly felt as if I had reclaimed an important piece of myself, of my spirit, that had been sorely missing. I realized that I had allowed my sense of humor, which had always mitigated the bad breaks in my life and enhanced the good ones, to fall victim to the machete my ex-husband had taken to my life. I determined right then that this was not acceptable to me. While I couldn't stop his rampant hacking away at much of the life we had built together, I would not allow him to take my sense of humor from me. I instinctively knew that humor was the most potent, and just about the only, protection I had at my disposal to survive the crises unfolding around me.

So now here I am, more than ten years older and I hope at least a little wiser than when I first started this collection of pineapple episodes. The storyline has certainly changed a lot since the beginning. My idea of what constitutes a "crisis" has evolved a bit as well. The tragedy of visible Spanx overflow kind of pales in comparison to personal devastation and financial ruin. (Although, Spanx overflow does remain a matter of some concern.) I also know very well that even what I now classify as a "real" crisis wouldn't even register on the screen of millions of other people. I am not living in a war zone or battling a terminal illness, as are so many others who daily endure such catastrophic conditions with incredible grace. I don't know why some suffer so greatly in this world. There certainly seems no rhyme or reason to the rain that falls on the just and unjust alike. I've done my share of railing against the capriciousness of life, yet I am not necessarily closer to understanding or explaining it. I am not even completely clear on the purpose, large or small, earthly or cosmic, that the dismantling of my own life served. It was certainly not the way I had planned it. Couldn't any lessons I needed to learn have been taught in a less devastating way? Did they really have to be so hands-on? Why not a virtual classroom; isn't distance learning all the rage?

I don't know why everything had to happen to me in the up-close-and-in-person way it did, but I do know this: we will all face some type of struggle, grand or mundane, at some point in our lives, and the more resilient among us will be better able to survive having all of our plans unexpectedly go south. I have found that humor can be a tremendous aid in developing resilience. While many of the unexpected situations I found myself in over the past ten years have been more absurd than humorous, laughing, even meagerly, at the absurdity often made me feel better than cursing or crying about it—although, as I said before, I took those approaches from time to time as well. Perhaps, if we can find a way to, if not laugh, at least sneak in a smile in the midst our worst times, we may gain just the momentum we need to not only bounce, but to keep bouncing back. So, in that spirit, I offer these various tales of laughter and tears as a toast to bouncing back—Spanx optional—no matter how far afield our pineapples may go!

1

Tears for Fears

AROUND 8:00 A.M. one Saturday morning in late February, 2002, my husband "Richard"—Dick to those who know him—and I were still asleep when the phone rang. I answered and heard my mother's quavering voice on the other end. I had been waiting to hear the results of my father's medical tests. My heart thumping out of my chest, I choked out the words, "It's not good news, is it, Mommy?"

"No, it's not," she cried. "Daddy has cancer, and it's already in his lungs and liver. There's nothing they can do," she murmured, her voice barely audible.

"No, no, no," is all I could manage to warble over and over again.

At this point Dick, who had been roused by the ring of the telephone and was showing at least preliminary interest in my emotional response, raised his eyebrows at me, a silent inquiry as to the nature of the call. I instinctively covered the mouthpiece of the receiver (as if shielding my mother from hearing the news spoken aloud again would make it less true) and whimpered, "My dad has cancer and it's very advanced."

His response? A disgusted "Oh, God" and then he rolled back over facing away from me, punching at his pillow and "harumphing" the way someone does when his sleep has been rudely invaded by a neighbor's barking dog or loud music or other such annoyance.

Let me be perfectly clear: I told my husband of 22 years that my father was dying and he responded, "Oh, God." Not as in "Oh, God, how horrible, this is devastatingly tragic news, please say there is some mistake." No, it was clearly "Oh, God" as in "for *that* you interrupted my sleep, what the hell does a guy have to do around here to get a little shuteye." If his tone left any doubt about his feelings, his rolling over and going back to sleep pretty much sealed the deal for me. There was no mistaking it—he was pissed. And rightfully so. After all, couldn't my father have shown a little consideration and gotten cancer during normal business hours? Did it really have to be early on a Saturday morning? And, come to think of it, what was the deal with my mother? I mean, if it was too late to do anything to save my dad, why the big urgency to call me first thing and awaken my husband? The nerve of some people.

It is impossible to say which stunned me more, the news about my father or Dick's reaction to it. His response was bizarre, even for him who comes from a long line of what I've always facetiously referred to as "inappropriate reactors." Apparently, a lack of appropriate emotions or, to give his family the benefit of the doubt, an inability to display appropriate emotions, is genetic. His father once called to tell me of the completely unexpected death of a beloved aunt with the following words: "Hey, guess what, Aunt Lucy died," in the same tone used for conveying mild surprise about having won $50 on a scratch-off lottery ticket. When I responded with a very shocked and upset, "What? Oh my God, I can't believe this," he just said, "Yeah, isn't that something?" as if we were talking about a freakish May snowfall. No, they didn't do strong emotion well.

Even so, taken together with the increasingly erratic nature of Dick's behavior during the past year or so, his "Oh, God" response registered with me as more than just his genetic predisposition for inappropriateness. This response took inappropriateness to a whole new level, but as much as I wanted to smack him over the head with the lamp and demand an explanation for his outrageous reaction that instant, I knew better than to call him on it. I hadn't gotten a satisfying explanation from him about anything more serious than why the air conditioner was making a whining sound in at least the past twelve months. When I had dared to ask about his detached and angry behavior any time in the past year, I was promptly rewarded with even more detachment and anger. And so, deciding it was wiser to let sleeping dogs lie—or, more accurately in retrospect, to let lying dogs sleep—I got out of bed to call my sisters from a different phone.

My conversations with my two older sisters were a babbling mishmash of fears and concerns about any possible treatment options, about my mother, about—oh, my God, deep breath here—funerals. This news had hit us all out of left field and none of us was able to digest it yet. But I had one more very specific concern that I didn't voice to them, hoping that not talking about it would make it go away. When I hung up the phone, it was clear my strategy had failed miserably. One singular unspoken thought was still pulsating in my brain: I was next on the list.

I am notorious for seeing connections where none exist, for "reading signs" where nothing has been written. My father had gone to his doctor the same week that I had had my annual mammogram. Both of us had received concerned calls from our doctors ordering follow-up tests. My father had just received his devastating results, and it stood to reason in my mind that my results were now a foregone conclusion. Although my tests were not scheduled for another week, I was sure my father's diagnosis was a foreshadowing of my own fate. My mind raced ahead to a news story headline in my hometown weekly newspaper, "Father and Daughter Diagnosed Together." I imagined conversations among people we knew commenting on the strange, sad coincidence.

Reinforcing my conviction about my diagnosis was the fact that I felt I had dodged that bullet many times in recent years and it seemed only logical to my convoluted way of thinking that my luck had run out. After all, I hadn't had a single mammogram in the past ten years that hadn't required follow-up action. My breasts had been man- (and woman-) handled by what seemed like 56 different pairs of hands from Atlanta to Chicago, as well as being subjected to countless

mammograms, sonograms and needle biopsies. Each time had ended up being a false alarm, thank God, but this time was different, I
thought. This time the bullet had my name on it, I was certain.

I mentally ran through the same laundry list of concerns I made
every time I awaited test results—everything from insurance deduct-
ibles to my pathological fear of throwing up to not being around long
enough to attend the college graduation of my 20-year-old daughter
Torrie. But this time, a whole new dimension of worry had been added. If I were sick, who would help my 84-year-old mother care for my
father? I thought back to the nightmare of in-hospital and home care
necessary when my father had had pneumonia and couldn't even
imagine what would be involved now. We were adding a colostomy,
chemotherapy and who-knew-what else to the mix...plus the knowledge that this time my father's journey was one of no return. I broke
down in huge gulping sobs and prayed that God would let me slip by
again, prayed that I would get a free pass one more time.

A couple of hours had passed since the phone call from my mother. I heard the shower running in my bathroom, so I assumed Sleeping
Beauty had risen from his slumber. I blew my nose and splashed
some cold water on my face in the kitchen sink. He emerged from the
bedroom, looked at me blankly and asked with annoyance, "What's
wrong with you?"

Oh, broke another damn nail, I wanted to reply. I'm pretty upset
about it. And, oh yeah, my father's dying and I'm afraid I might be too.

What I really said was, "What do you *think* is wrong?"

He shrugged a kind of acknowledgement, told me he had to go to
the office for the rest of the day and left. I took the dog, drove to the
park and cried for four miles on the trail around the lake. It was an
overcast winter day, but I kept my sunglasses on and walked with my
head down, hoping to avoid anyone I knew. As I walked, I tried to gain
some kind of perspective on the topsy-turvy turns my life had taken in
a relatively short period of time. Just a couple of years earlier, full of
the excitement and anticipation of a new beginning, Dick, Torrie and
I had moved from Atlanta to Chicago to accommodate Dick's new

promotion. Six months after we got there, Dick was "downsized" out of his position. Well, that was the face-saving term we used because in truth he had been fired. It was certainly an unexpected blow to him, but, fortunately, he was well-known in his industry and was offered another very good job in short order—back in Atlanta. So, Dick returned to Atlanta immediately while Torrie and I stayed behind in Chicago to finish up her school quarter and sell the house.

Once reunited in Atlanta, we more than made up for any loss of togetherness by shoehorning ourselves into the tiny apartment that served as our temporary living quarters while our new house was being built, a process that ran a full seven months over the projected timeline and definitely past the expiration date on our tolerance for living so cozily. Finally, however, we moved into our house and began resettling into our lives in Atlanta, just in time to see Torrie off to her freshman year in college. It seemed to me that life was just getting back to normal when Dick came home from the office a little early one afternoon and, walking by me as I worked at the computer keyboard, "mentioned" that he had made an important decision, one he'd been mulling for a while, but had failed to share with me until that very moment. He had decided, he said, to quit his job and partner with a colleague to begin a new business from scratch, one he knew very little about. Shock does not begin to describe my reaction. My loud protestations and desperate pleading not to jump off this cliff, taking our entire future security with him, fell on deaf ears, as he was determined to make his mark in this way. In his mind, he was taking the bull of his destiny by the horns. He was clearly on a mission, and I knew from experience that there was no talking him out of it. I tried to rein in my panic—more like sheer terror—and reassure myself that neither he nor his partner, a very successful businessman, was completely insane and that, therefore, they must know what they were doing. I also acknowledged that I was not necessarily the best judge of the wisdom of any business plan as the three words that best describe me are: Financially Risk Averse. I'm the kind of person who would have told Steve Jobs to quit tinkering around in his garage and get a sensible job waiting tables. So, I tried to keep the faith, but in the up-and-down two years since Dick's folly had begun, the only results I had seen were his increasingly evasive answers about the financial status of the business along with his increasingly troubling behavior. If I dared broach either subject with him, he shut me down immediately and stormed off.

I was long used to his moodiness and periods of withdrawal, but the new level of detachment he'd been displaying for the previous several months, capped off by his stunning reaction (or lack thereof) to my father's diagnosis that morning, was beyond the pale. Even I, who knew his complicated and troubled back story and routinely gave him a wide emotional berth because of it, was at a loss to comprehend this extreme response, much less disposed to excuse it. In the past year he seemed to have completely reverted to the distant and defensive behavior he had routinely displayed in the early years of our marriage. His indifference toward me back then was so complete that I was sure he wouldn't have cared or even noticed if I had packed up and left him. And only ten months after our wedding, I was close to doing just that…until I realized that the daily bouts of nausea I had been suffering, which I had naively attributed to carsickness, were, in fact, heralding the biggest and best news of my life—one little Miss Torrie was quite unexpectedly on the way.

But as difficult as those early years with Dick had been, as he matured and grew more secure, the good guy I had always stubbornly insisted was hiding deep inside his pain and fear seemed to emerge and take control. For long stretches of time in our marriage I believed I was happy, or at least happy enough. After all, whose marriage is without compromise? I truly thought Dick had beaten his demons and he did such a good job of convincing me that I eventually came to trust him completely and rely on his support. But in the past year or so, it had become a painful episode of déjà vu. The good guy had left the building, and I felt absolutely helpless to coax him back despite how much I needed and wanted to.

Walking on, my thoughts shifted to my father. It just seemed impossible that he was dying. It had been just over two months since he'd been at my house for Christmas. Oh, thank God I had driven up to Pennsylvania to bring him and my mother to Atlanta for the holidays, I thought. It was only three months post-9/11 then and my mother had refused to get aboard an airplane, so I made the 1,400-mile round-trip to retrieve them. The strong urge I had felt to push them to come for Christmas took on a sense of divine inspiration as I reflected back. To persuade them, I had joked at the time that we didn't know how many Christmases they had left. Of course, given their relatively robust health, that's what it was—a joke. None of us ever imagined how the picture would shift a few months later, for my father...and possibly for me, I couldn't help thinking.

The anxiety of the next several days as my father prepared for surgery and I for my follow-up tests was unbearable. (Why do they call you with the scary news that you need additional testing for a "suspicious" finding and then make you wait *two excruciating weeks* to get it? Even if the tests finally reveal that you are in the clear, by then you have been laced up in a straitjacket and are unable to applaud the news.) I knew better than to expect any comfort at home and turned to my friends for support. With their help, I had been holding up fairly well. That is, until the day before my tests. I awoke that morning to a pretty serious panic attack. The kind where your heartbeat thunders in your ears, your thoughts are disjointed and you feel as if you are going to jump out of your skin. It is a thoroughly discomfiting feeling, and if you have never suffered such an episode, consider yourself generously blessed. The only way I can describe it is to say you feel a profound lack of safety, not in your specific surroundings or situation, but in your very being. The threat you sense, the danger you instinctively want to flee is not coming from without, but within. Your impulse is to "scramble to safety," but there is nowhere to scramble to (or from, for that matter).

I was pacing deliberately through the rooms in my house, focusing on regulating my breathing and trying desperately to talk myself down from the ledge when the phone rang. I forced myself to take and release one more deep breath before answering, hoping that would allow me to speak without sounding like a crazed lunatic. When I picked up the phone, I was momentarily taken aback by the unfamiliar voice on the other end. After a few seconds, I realized it was Jorge, a former student from the adult English as a Second Language classes that I taught.

Oh, shoot, our meeting, I thought to myself. In the chaos of the past several days, I had completely forgotten that weeks earlier I'd agreed to meet him this very morning to proofread his resume. Trying to cover for my memory lapse, I stumbled around for a few seconds and finally lied through my teeth, insisting that of course I had remembered our appointment and even added that I was all but ready to leave the house to meet him. ("All but ready," as soon as my heart palpitations, hyperventilating and profuse perspiring stopped, that is. As soon as I could form one complete thought.) I hoped the embarrassed stumbling over my words would be lost in translation and that he wouldn't guess that correcting his resume was the last thing on my mind. I hung up the phone and ran to get dressed. Looking at my reflection in the mirror as I ran a brush through my hair, I made a surprising discovery—my hands were no longer shaking. While I had expected to be filled with dread at having to leave the house, I realized I was actually feeling calmer. Maybe it would do me good to have something else to focus on for a little while, I decided, as I grabbed my keys and headed out the door.

I had first met Jorge several months earlier when he had been a student in one of my classes. I had been trying in vain ever since to fix him up with my sister. I thought back to the first conversation my sister and I had had about him.

"There's a handsome Colombian man in my new class that I think you might like," I told my sister.

"Does he meet the minimum requirements?" she asked.

"You mean, does he have a pulse? Yes, he does. Well, okay, I haven't actually felt it for myself, but I'm assuming since he's walking upright and breathing, he does in fact have one," I replied.

"You're probably right," she agreed and then added rather dreamily, "mmm, walking upright, breathing and he has a pulse—yes, just my type."

With her permission (and not so much as a wink or a nod to him) I had orchestrated several "accidental" meetings between them. A party at my house, dinner after class, even a shopping trip to select art supplies. Alas, something had always gone wrong at the last minute, and the two of them still hadn't met each other. I hadn't cooked up any schemes recently because Jorge's work schedule had changed and he was no longer taking classes at my school. In spite of the present grim circumstances, I couldn't help but smile a little as I remembered the silly conversations my sister and I had had just a few months ago. How quickly and dramatically life changes, I thought. Immediately I could feel myself beginning the familiar slide down the slippery slope of "whys" and "what ifs" into the tarry pit of despair.

"No!" I actually said aloud to myself, blinking back the tears. "You cannot go there, not now, not if you want to maintain enough composure to even back out of the driveway." I forced myself to think one positive thought. I willed myself to see the grace in the smallest and most incidental gestures of life. Like this meeting with Jorge today, I thought to myself. Perhaps it was the hand of fate, providing a temporary, but much needed distraction from my worries. And maybe, just maybe, I thought, it was fate's hand giving me another chance to play matchmaker.

Walking through the door of the little cafe, I spotted Jorge sitting at a table in the corner. He stood up to greet me as I approached and gave me a half embrace with one arm as he pulled the chair out for me with the other. I picked up the vaguest hint of his aftershave as I brushed by him to sit down and quite unexpectedly felt my senses sort of snap to, as if I had just inhaled smelling salts instead of aftershave. A short but sharp pang of longing shot through me. A vapor of a memory—the intoxicating scent of Polo on Dick's smooth-shaven cheek sending a shiver down my spine. A scent and a sensation both too long absent. Enough of that, I silently scolded myself, focus on the task at hand!

As I sat down, Jorge, still standing, asked what he could get me to drink or eat. He attended to me as if I were a guest in his home instead of a customer in a coffee shop. I accepted a diet Coke (it had been seventeen minutes since my last one and I didn't need to add withdrawal symptoms to my already precarious mental state), but I wasn't about to risk introducing food to my flip-flopping stomach here in public. But, he was insistent that I eat *something*, so I settled on a sesame bagel. When I reached for my wallet to give him a couple dollars to pay for my order, he shooed me away, saying, "It is my pleasure. You are very kind with me, for help me with my resume." I didn't know if it was his accent, his misphrasing or possibly the barometric pressure, but I felt an odd tremble inside. It was gone as fast as it came.

Upon bringing my order back to the table, he set the paper plate down in front of me with a small flourish. He then carefully folded and laid out a paper napkin, topped it with a plastic knife and proceeded to remove the paper wrapper from my straw before positioning it through the plastic lid of my cup. He repeated the process at his place setting. I watched in fascination as he repositioned a flower in the bud vase on the table and plucked two wilted leaves from it.

"Much better," he murmured.

You would have thought he was preparing for a state dinner, but I could tell from his offhand manner that this kind of attention to detail was nothing out of the ordinary for him. When I asked if he was expecting any of the crowned heads of Europe to join us, he laughed and explained that just because the tableware was rather inelegant was no reason for people's habits to match it. (Oh no, I suddenly thought, he can never find out about the time my college roommate and I ate potato salad out of the container with our fingers because we were too lazy to wash a dish and a fork. Something like that could definitely hurt my sister's chances with him.)

We chatted for a few minutes while I picked at the sesame seeds on my bagel with my fingernail. I was sure I was violating some international etiquette law, but he graciously pretended not to notice. Finally, he cleared the table and I started looking over his resume. Wow! I knew that he was well-educated, but I hadn't realized to what extent. He held three degrees, had worked in top-level finance and marketing positions on two continents and had traveled to nearly every country on the globe. All that, plus a pulse. Just wait till my sister heard this!

Jorge filled in some details about his background and experience while I tweaked a couple sections of his resume. I undangled a participle here, brokered a subject/verb agreement there and, *voila`*, it was good to go. I handed him back his monogrammed Mont Blanc pen—thank goodness he'd slipped it into my hand before I'd embarrassed myself further by pulling out the purple plastic pen I'd picked up at the dry cleaners. As he excused himself to the men's room, I glanced at my watch and was surprised to see that nearly two hours had passed. I felt much steadier than when I'd walked in the door. I guess a short respite had done me good, I thought. I felt calmer and more clearheaded than I had in days. I told myself that I was going to get through everything that was facing me. It was unbearable to think of my dad in pain, frightened and dying. It was impossible to imagine saying good-bye to him, but I just repeated to myself that I would somehow find the strength, even without Dick's familiar shoulder to lean on, to do whatever I had to do. "Grown-ups do hard things. You are a grown-up. You can do hard things," I murmured, mantra-like.

I stood by the door, waiting for Jorge to come back from the bathroom so I could say good-bye and go. Just as he was walking toward me, my cell phone rang. I answered and it was someone from the hospital, asking if I could come in an hour early for my appointment the next day because my doctor wanted the radiologist herself to be there to read the films on the spot. It was all the motivation I needed to completely forget my shaky resolve. My two-hour escape was over. My stomach roiled, my knees went weak and I all but collapsed to the floor in tears. Jorge came rushing up to see what had happened. I kept blubbering, "Nothing," but for some reason he didn't believe me.

He ushered me to a chair where I'm sure I shattered every convention of decorum that Elizabeth Post—or her Colombian counterpart—ever dreamed of by crying and heaving within close proximity of a dining surface. Instantly, Jorge reached into his pocket, retrieved a freshly laundered and pressed handkerchief and placed it in my hand. I felt that deep trembling sensation again. Fleeting, but discernible. He gave me the handkerchief so I could blow my nose, but I hesitated, not feeling altogether comfortable using the expensive-looking square of linen for so lowly a task. In the end I figured it was better to soil his fancy hanky than to let my nose drip (or use my sleeve). Of course, by then I had to tell him everything that was going on, how destroyed I was about my father's diagnosis and how petrified I was about my own. He listened attentively, but I wasn't sure how many details he really got between my gulping and sniffling and the language barrier. Apparently, he had a general idea of the situation because he just kept saying over and over "I'm so sorry, I'm so sorry." (Although it's possible he meant he was so sorry he had ever asked me to help him.) When I was finally able to breathe normally, he suggested that I call Dick to meet me because he didn't think it was a good idea for me to drive when I was so upset. I actually snorted in response. (Good thing I had blown my nose in his hanky after all or that would have been one embarrassingly messy snort.) And, P.S., I thought, what man of my generation carries a monogrammed white linen handkerchief in his pocket? The only man I'd seen carry a white, albeit cotton, hanky as part of his daily attire was my dad, and that memory made me puddle up again.

Paralyzing waves of fear and anxiety washed over me once more, leaving me unable to move from the chair. Embarrassed, I urged him to go, saying that I was just going to sit there for a few minutes to regain my composure, although I believe my composure was in another time zone by that point. Any minute, I thought to myself, he's going to ask me how to get his teacher evaluation form back from the school so he can add "complete nut job" under the "Comments" section.

In the end, he stayed and talked with me for another hour, almost up until the time I had to leave to teach my evening class. I felt awful because I knew this was his only day off and there he was saddled with a lunatic who not only babbled nonsensically, but babbled non-sensically in a language he didn't fully comprehend. I appreciated his distracting me from the crisis at hand, but I felt certain he was only being kind to the mentally unstable. Well, I'll reward him with my sister and then we'll be even, I thought, pathologically uncomfortable with the idea of having any outstanding debts. By the time I left for class, I felt in control of myself again. And I felt something else that I couldn't put my finger on, something that seemed to penetrate me, yet was indefinable.

In the car, different images from the afternoon collided in my head: Jorge standing to greet me, pulling out the chair for me and handing me his handkerchief, to say nothing of his sacrificing his af-ternoon to babysit me. At a red light in front of Walgreen's, it hit me. It was about *care*. I'd felt *cared for*. The more I thought about it, the more I realized that everything about Jorge's actions from wearing co-logne to folding the napkins to straightening the flower vase bespoke the care that he showed for himself, for his surroundings, and today, by accident, for me. Oh, my gosh, I thought, *that's* what had reso-nated so deeply within me. Someone had exhibited simple caring behavior towards me. It had been so long since I'd felt cared for, no wonder I hadn't recognized it at first. Now that I had, I was overcome with emotion, as if being reunited with a long-lost relative. I hadn't realized until that moment how much a sense of being cared for had been missing from my life and how thoroughly I had tried to protect myself from acknowledging its absence. It was painful to admit that I was so perniciously starved for care as to be overwhelmed by ges-tures of basic human decency. I thought of a recent conversation I'd had with my friend Suzi that in retrospect seemed pathetic and em-barrassing. I'd called her excited about what I took as a hopeful sign regarding Dick's behavior toward me.

"I had about 100 final tests to correct," I had told her, "and when I asked Dick if he would help by reading the answer key to me, he actually did it!" I was practically gushing.

"And?" she'd asked, waiting to hear something to justify my excitement.

"And? And nothing. Didn't you hear me?" I'd responded. "He did it. He helped me. For, like, 45 minutes. I think he's coming around."

How humiliating it seemed now. Squirrels in the park were tossed bigger scraps than that.

I arrived at my class and was glad to have something concrete to do as there were too many thoughts jumbled up in my head. I picked up my class materials from the office and took them to my room. A few of the other teachers and I had made plans to take our students out for pizza on this last night of class. While the mood of the last day of a term is always celebratory, tonight's celebration would be bitter-sweet, I thought. Not just because of what was going on in my personal life, but because I had grown especially attached to this group. We had been together for almost six months and had developed a real bond. They had been to my house for a Christmas party (one of the many failed opportunities I'd arranged for Jorge and my sister to meet) and a baby shower. We had commiserated over unwelcome birthdays, bad bosses and sick babies for the past two terms. I had even told them about my father and about my "suspicious" mammogram. It was going to be sad to say good-bye to them.

After I had handed back the final exams and congratulated each of them on their hard work and achievement, one young woman raised her hand. When I asked her what she needed, she stood and said, "We want you to know that we love you and that we are all praying for you and your father." Everyone else chimed in as she spoke, telling me how concerned they were about me and how certain they were that I was going to be fine. And then I witnessed the most moving and humbling display as every student in the room, Christian, Buddhist, Muslim and, for all I know, Druid, bowed their heads, closed their eyes and said a silent prayer for me. Waterproof mascara certainly proved itself to be one of my better choices that day. When I stopped sobbing that time, I gathered my things and we left for the pizza party.

When I got home, Dick was in bed watching TV. A few days earlier, in one of his increasingly rare moments of decency, he had promised to go with me to the hospital. I told him about the phone call and that we needed to be there an hour earlier than originally planned.

"You'll still get to sleep in a little bit later than when you get up for work," I offered as compensation.

He replied that he would not be staying home and going to the hospital with me. He explained that his plan was to get up early, go to the office for a couple of hours and then drive back home to go to the hospital with me. Considering that Atlanta traffic made that outing at least a two-hour round trip, I couldn't see the sense in this plan, but he insisted that he needed to be at the office. He also insisted that he knew he "should" go with me and he swore he would be back home in time. I didn't understand why he couldn't work from home that morning and eliminate all the extra driving, but it seemed as if he was trying to make amends for his usual disinterest, so I let it go.

"But," I said, accustomed to his missed deadlines and weak follow-through even on his good days, "you absolutely have to be here on time. I can't be late."

"No problem," he said.

I was naive enough at that point to mistake solicitude born of guilt for genuine concern and, in light of the afternoon's events, was a little heartened at his desire to "take care of me." I thought back to his "good guy" days and of how truly concerned he'd been at different times over the years when I'd had "suspicious" findings. One time he'd stayed with me, holding my hand, through the surgeon's nerve-wracking exam and another time he'd demanded to speak with the radiologist personally (though we'd been told it was not possible) and refused to leave the hospital until we did. Yet one more time I thought ruefully how times change. But, maybe they could change back again, I silently prayed. I needed them to change back.

The next morning, Dick did indeed get up very early and go to work, and that's pretty much where the success of his plan ended. I called him when I woke up and he assured me he'd be home on time and instructed me to wait for him. I waited and waited and waited, but he was nowhere in sight. Every time I called his cell phone, I got his voice mail. I was getting down to the final few moments when I needed to leave in order to get to the hospital on time. I called his cell one more time and got him. He said he was running late, that he would meet me at the hospital. He estimated we would arrive at the same time. When I walked into the waiting room at the hospital, he wasn't there yet. I checked in, filled out the paperwork, handed it in and he wasn't there yet. I went into one of the admissions cubicles, gave a clerk all my insurance information, came out and he wasn't there yet. I sat nervously fidgeting with my purse and adjusting my watchband for about ten minutes and he wasn't there yet. The technologist called me in for my tests and he still wasn't there. Classic Dick, I couldn't help thinking, big plans and broken promises. I went in for my tests alone.

The technologist explained to me that she was going to do a few diagnostic mammograms, close-ups of the suspicious spot, and then the radiologist would look at them to decide if we needed to go further. I knew the drill. Smash. Squish. Repeat. After she finished, she sent me to the dressing room to wait. Once there, my eyes landed on an assortment of fashion magazines fanned out on a coffee table. How absurd that display seemed to me. I couldn't imagine anyone really kicking back and relaxing here with a copy of "Allure" while awaiting a potentially un-alluring fate. Still, when nervously picking at my acrylic nails proved an insufficient distraction, I broke down and picked up a recent issue from the collection. I must have scanned the story headlines on the front cover at least ten times without comprehending a single word. I set it back down, my sweating hands smearing ink all over some *über* model's flawlessly airbrushed complexion. Deal with it, chick, I thought!

The door opened (my heart lurched to my throat) and the technologist said the radiologist had seen the films, "wasn't happy," and now wanted an ultrasound.

"That doesn't sound good," I ventured anxiously.

"No, it just means that she wasn't satisfied with the image and wants to get a better look," she answered too cheerily.

I didn't believe a word. I closed my eyes for the duration of the ultrasound. I would have closed my ears too if that were possible. I didn't want to see the screen or the technologist's expression. I didn't want to hear (and try to interpret) any "hmm's" or "aha's." I just wanted it to be over. When it was, I was dispatched back to the dressing room where I was free to wreak further sweaty havoc on the perfect skin of anorectic models.

I was counting the ceiling tiles for the third time when the door swung open again. This time the technologist sounded sincere when she proclaimed with a smile, "Dr. Cruise says, 'go home,' and she'll see you next year!"

"I'm okay?" I asked, not convinced yet.

"Yes, you are. It's just another cyst, actually two on top of each other, so it looked strange. You're good to go."

I felt my body go as limp as a rag doll with relief. I thanked her profusely for the good news, got dressed in a flash and headed out to the waiting room where I hoped Dick would finally be. I pushed the door open and looked around expectantly, no husband visible. I walked out into the room and spied him sitting in a chair off to the side. He was slumped down, *sound asleep.* So glad he'd been able to overcome his anxiety about my test results. I so hated causing him undue mental anguish. I nudged him. He opened his eyes lazily and stared up at me.

"Oh, hey," he said groggily.

"Hey, yourself," I said. "I'm okay,"

"Yeah, so, how were your tests," he asked as if inquiring about my SAT scores.

"Good. Well, not good as in enjoyable, but fine. I mean I'm fine. Everything's okay."

"Well, that's good," he said.

I suggested we have lunch together, but he said he needed to get back to work. He never really did explain why he had been so late except to say that traffic had been bad. We walked out of the door of the hospital. He gave me a quick peck on the lips and we parted, walking in opposite directions to our parked cars. Once alone inside my car, it was hard not to think about the sharp contrast between my experiences the day before with Jorge and my students and this day with Dick. A cold rain began to fall and I stared out at the gray skies, feeling alone, isolated and abandoned. Then I remembered that just minutes ago I had been making silent bargains with God for my life and I shot a glance heavenward and whispered, "Thank you." We humans have such short memories and generally ungrateful hearts. Yes, I was immensely grateful for the good test results. And I was also very grateful for the care and concern shown me in recent days by my friends and students, but human that I am, I wanted something more; I wanted that care and concern to come from my husband. I shot another glance heavenward.

"Please," I uttered in a small voice, "just this one thing more. Please."

I sat in silence for a moment or two, as if expecting to hear an answer. None came, so I turned the key in the ignition and drove home alone.

2

The Mourning After

MY FATHER DIED on Monday, May 13, 2002. I began mourning for him three months to the day later on Monday, August 13. A more unlikely trigger for my grief I can't imagine: Carole King singing "Been to Canaan" on my car radio. I feel confident saying that my dad lived his 82½ years on earth without having the slightest clue who Carole King was or having knowingly listened to her music. You would be hard-pressed to find the slimmest connection between this song and my dad. A great student of history, if not religion, my dad surely could have located the historical "Canaan" on a map, but that was hardly a cause for tears. The more metaphorical aspects of longing to return a promised land represented by Canaan would likely have little affected my dad, a man not given to introspection, who prized the concrete above the abstract, the literal above the figurative, the future above the past. The song and my father were irrelevant to each other on every level, it seemed. In retrospect, I realize any armchair analyst could have put the pieces together without breaking much of a psychological sweat, but at that moment—furiously blinking the tears away to navigate the intersection without running over anyone—it seemed incongruous yet utterly debilitating to me.

The scant eighty days between my father's diagnosis and his death slipped through my fingers with the slickness of quicksilver. Not since my first days as a new mother, reveling in my infant daughter's every coo and cry, had I tried so desperately to stop time and hold it in my hands. And not since then had the ache of falling short been so pervasive. The first and last days of life, the bookends of our human existence, are such slender slivers of time. They inevitably pass too swiftly, leaving many a tender wish for the future or treasured memory of the past still resting on our lips, unspoken.

After I learned that my dad was dying, the hours in a day seemed to shrink while the physical distance between us seemed to grow. Life seemed to be moving in 2/2 time, and I struggled to keep pace from 700 miles away. Less than a day after my dad's diagnosis of metastatic colon cancer, he was scheduled for surgery, so dangerously was his bowel obstructed. The surgeon was direct and firm. I read him loud and clear, even from five states away. My father needed surgery ASAP to prevent his colon from perforating and causing deadly peritonitis. It was premature to debate various cancer treatment protocols and prognoses of weeks versus months, explained the surgeon, when my father's colon might well rupture (actually, the surgeon said "explode") at any moment and quite possibly kill him on the spot. Obviously, the immediate threat had to be addressed before any longer-range plans could be outlined. Thus, was my obstinate, recalcitrant, *testa dura* of a father admitted to the hospital and prepped for surgery. After 24-hours of hospital-supervised "bowel cleansing," my father was ready for surgery early the following morning. I am still not clear on the precise unfolding of events, but apparently, there was some sort of delay in the surgeon's schedule that morning, during which time my notoriously impatient and hungry father determined he would be better off (and certainly better fed) waiting at home. So he checked himself out, got in his car and drove home. I am not kidding you. He did this. With a ticking time bomb in his abdomen and a hospital bracelet on his wrist, my dad up and left, as if he'd been standing in line at the bakery and had decided the donuts weren't worth the wait. Don't bother to gape in disbelief and demand why the nurses, the doctors, my mother or *someone* didn't do something to stop him. Trust me, there was nothing to be done. Not when my dad set his mind on something. He was a steamroller. If you weren't on board, you jumped out of the way—*that* was the only thing to be done. The surgeon, of course, failed to take my dad's stunt so easily in stride. When he was informed, his anger and incredulity clearly registered, again, from five states—likely even five *planets*—away!

And, yet, as insanely reckless and wrong-headed as it was for my dad to check himself out on the cusp of urgently needed surgery, that day turned out to be a gift of quieting and sustaining grace for him and my mother. They spent the day together, listening to Dean Martin and Jerry Vale albums and looking through photos, reliving 58 years of shared memories. They held onto each other all day, laughing, crying, feeling grateful, feeling cheated. Toward evening, a few relatives came by and the reminiscing continued, a comforting glow displacing the chilling shadows of late winter. The next morning, my dad checked himself back into the hospital, and nothing was ever, ever the same again.

Looking back now, the day my dad went rogue seems even more of a blessing. I think we all had the general impression that following the surgery to head off deadly peritonitis, my father would go home and things would be "normal" for a while. Up until the instant the scalpel rent that curtain in two, he still seemed so, well, normal. Not at all like a sick man, certainly not a terminally sick man. That illusion shattered with the surgeon's first stroke. Any notion of life returning to "normal," even if only temporarily, was excised as thoroughly as my father's diseased colon. There would be no reprieve, no respite, no going home even for a day, not this time. The grueling surgery, which exchanged a large portion of my dad's intestines for a colostomy bag, left him with a visibly, irreversibly compromised body. And one other thing, something wholly unanticipated: an inexplicable, unflappable belief that he was not going to die.

Between the time I first visited my father in the hospital and the day he died, he never, to my knowledge, made any reference to his dying. Everything he said was framed in terms of "when he was better" or "when he went home." I don't know if it was massive denial or if he truly didn't grasp the timeline he was facing. And, to be honest, that suited me—one part Pollyanna and three parts coward—just fine because I was nothing short of terrified to face my dad with the dark cloud of his certain death suspended between us. I didn't know how to do that. How should I act, what should I say? I had no idea.

Certainly, in the past few years I had kept more than one vigil at my father's hospital bedside. Twice in recent times, wicked and defiant strains of pneumonia had wracked his system mercilessly for days on end, nudging him, limp and depleted, closer and closer to death's doorstep. In the midst of one siege, when the medical staffs of two separate hospitals had exhausted all their resources, a soft-spoken pulmonologist pulled me aside.

"I want you to know we have thrown all we have at this infection for two weeks," he stated soberly. "Please understand that it is now a waiting game to see who gives up first, the pneumonia or your father's immune system."

I nodded solemnly in acknowledgement, as a breath caught in my throat and a tear rolled down my cheek. Yet, as serious as that situation was, as gravely ill as my father was at that point, death was not inevitable; despite the unfavorable odds, we could all walk into my dad's room, look him squarely in the eye and tell him he was not yet defeated, that his fight against a tenacious and formidable opponent was still winnable.

That same afternoon my father looked over at me through fever-weary, half-closed eyes and sighed heavily. "Are they going to take me out and shoot me?" he asked half joking, half pleading. "Do they still shoot sick horses?"

"Maybe they do," I replied, "but not stubborn mules, so you are safe. You have no choice but to fight this and win."

We all figured he was on the road to winning the day that a psychiatric resident stopped by for a consult. My dad had been quite disoriented at some points during the worst of his illness (once thinking he was in prison!), and given my dad's age of 81, we all thought it was a good idea to rule out dementia or other problems. The resident introduced himself and my dad replied, "What do you mean psychiatrist, who the hell thinks I'm nuts?"

The resident proceeded to ask my dad the usual questions, i.e., did he know his name, did he know where he was (he answered hospital this time, not prison!) and then the doctor asked my dad if he knew what day it was.

"Monday," answered my dad correctly.

"Can you tell me anything else about the day?" continued the doctor, fishing for the exact date.

"Well, hell, yeah, it's V-E Day!" exclaimed my dad.

The resident—who looked about 12 years old—regarded my dad with a mixture of confusion and concern. It was clear he had no clue what my dad was talking about.

"It's V-E Day," my dad repeated louder, with a definite "duh" in his tone. "Victory in Europe. May 8. 1945. 55 years ago today." He paused between each phrase, as if giving the doctor clues.

"Oh, yes, right, I wasn't thinking," the resident said, convincing no one. He declared my father to have no dementia and swiftly bade us good-bye.

As soon as he had gone, my dad let us have it. "That kid doesn't even know what V-E Day is and you girls think *I'm* the one who's nuts," he declared. "That's pretty damn good."

This time around, of course, there was no "could," only a devastating "would." And the difference between "could die" and "would die" reduced me to a quivering coward, a lost and frightened child who was not equal to the adult task being demanded of her. My sister and I drove all night through a raging thunderstorm that spanned the entire 700-mile trip to be with my father shortly after his surgery. We arrived at the hospital, disheveled and distraught, and took the elevator to his floor. With each leaden footstep I took toward his room, my sense of dread grew and threatened to send me running in the opposite direction.

I needn't have fretted so. Walking into his room and forcing a cheery, "Hi, Daddy," we were met with a decidedly wan, but still heartfelt greeting in return. We stayed with him all afternoon, and every afternoon for the next week, and never once did he mention death, his or anyone else's. Our constant chatter lent an apparent buoyancy to the mood, but the space surrounding our words, the space that outlined every single letter of every single word, was sodden with sadness. And just when I felt my heart would break under weight of it—watching him sleep after he'd nodded off—he'd come alive and spout out some kooky "daddyism" that would lighten the load considerably.

"Now that's a damn shame!" he exclaimed on one such occasion, while pointing at the wall opposite his bed. Ever the builder, his eye had caught sight of a crooked outlet plate. "Can you believe that? A beautiful new building like this and that plate isn't square. It's a damn shame," he repeated, shaking his head with disgust.

Yes, it was truly scandalous; how could I not have noticed it myself?! How, he continued, could anyone have been so careless, especially on a tiled wall where it was obvious that the plate was not level with the grout lines? He was so incensed I thought he was going to demand an electrician come and straighten the offending outlet box that very instant. There he was, lying on his deathbed, hooked up to an assortment of monitors, IV tubes going in, a colostomy bag catching what came out, and he was up in arms about shoddy workmanship! That's how my dad made it very easy to sit with a dying man.

At the end of that initial week, I had to leave, but spent the following two months traveling by plane, car and ox cart when necessary between my home in Atlanta and my father's sickbed in Pennsylvania. I used personal and sick days to cobble together as many long weekends as I could without losing my job. Each time I went to the hospital, and later the nursing home, I felt the same queasy, resistant tugging in my stomach right before I arrived, afraid of what awaited me, afraid of not being able to handle it. And every single time, I was confounded by his good spirits and relatively "healthy" appearance. It was not a brave front for my benefit. I learned he had been holding court with family and old friends nearly every day since arriving at the nursing home. At other times, he was on the phone or joking with the nurses. This was in addition to having my mother there with him every day. How could this be?

The entire team of physicians at the hospital, from the surgeon to the radiologist to the oncologist, had made it very clear before my father was discharged: physically, he had reached the end of the road. The cancer had not only consumed his colon, but had deeply invaded his liver and had begun its assault on his lungs. In addition, he had lost the use of his legs, another debilitating side effect of the cancer that I hadn't realized would happen. He had little time left and, given his increasing care needs, they emphasized, allowing him to go home was unwise.

"We will, of course, do everything we can to make him as comfortable as possible," the oncologist assured me before my father was discharged. "His primary care physician will manage his care at the nursing home."

So, determined to get to the bottom of this mystery, I called his primary care doctor. I thought about asking him flat out, "Hey, is my dad really dying, or what?" but I settled for a more reasonable query.

"Is it the strong pain medication that has him feeling so…so… good?" I asked. (I wanted to add, "Because, if it is, I want some *pronto*!)

"Actually, he replied as he exhaled heavily, "your father is not on very strong pain medication."

"What do you mean he's not strong on pain meds? Why not?" I fairly demanded. I was all prepared to inform him that my parents had excellent insurance coverage, if that was the issue!

"Because he is not in any great pain, and, quite frankly, it's a bit of a puzzle. Your father's liver is absolutely *packed* with tumors, and he should be in a lot of pain, yet he isn't," he explained. "His only complaint is about not being able to walk and I've explained to him that there is nothing we can do about that."

I was speechless. How could he not be on strong pain medication at this point in his illness, how could he not *need* it? But, when

I thought about it, the doctor was right; the only thing my dad ever asked me about this care or condition was when the doctor was going to "do something for his legs." With spring upon us, my dad was concerned to the point of agitation that his yard and garden were not being taken care of. He wanted to get his flowers in the ground and didn't know how he could do that if he couldn't walk. I always answered this concern by telling him not worry, that my cousin Eric was taking good care of his yard. Still, I knew how desperately he wanted to see his yard and flowers in bloom one last time, so I even asked his doctor if there were any way we could take my dad on the less-than-half-mile trip.

"Despite appearances to the contrary," the doctor answered sympathetically, but with finality, "he really is very fragile and cannot be moved." So that was that, and it hurt deeply that we couldn't give my dad one thing he truly wanted.

The last time I was ever to see my father was a Saturday morning. I had arranged a stopover in Pennsylvania on a business trip between Atlanta and Chicago. It was a glorious May morning, warm and bright. A storybook morning, with trees budding, flowers blooming and birds chirping. When I walked into my dad's room, he was sitting up in bed, beaming more brightly that the springtime sun.

"Did you hear the news?" he asked excitedly, in a voice that was strong and clear. "Can you believe it?"

I had no idea what he was talking about and told him to slow down and tell me what was going on.

"Didn't anybody tell you? I walked! Isn't that something?" he continued with the pure joy of a child on Christmas morning.

At first I thought that maybe, for some unexpected reason, the nurses had gotten him out of bed and that he had interpreted that as "walking."

"You should have seen me. No one could here get over it," he continued. "I walked all over the place. I walked down to the house and all around the yard and you were right, Eric's doing a good job. The geraniums are starting to take off and the impatiens look good.

Boy, isn't the grass green? It's all the rain we had this year."

You could have lit a small village with the wattage from his smile. I played right along, expressing my surprise and happiness.

"And, son of a gun," he said with disappointment, "now this afternoon I can't move my legs. But, boy oh boy, it sure felt good to walk again." His voice trailed off and his eyes had a faraway look, as if focused on something in the distance that I couldn't see. If the word "bittersweet" hadn't already existed, I would have coined it right then and there, as joy and sorrow mingled in the tears spilling down my cheeks. A storybook morning indeed.

I kissed my dad good-bye late that Saturday afternoon and went on to Chicago. On Monday, shortly after noon, my sister called to tell me that our father—Daddy—was gone. I was standing in the hotel lobby when I took the call on my cell phone. I had just shared my father's "walking story" with the desk clerk. We'd become friendly during my many stays at this hotel. After I hung up, she asked me if everything was all right.

"That was my sister," I replied quietly. "My father passed away about 20 minutes ago."

"Oh, my, I am so sorry," she said with genuine sympathy.

"Thanks," I said. "So am I."

I stood there silently for a few seconds and then started walking to the elevator. Just as the bell dinged, I turned and called over my shoulder to her.

"He's gone, but you know what?"

"What?" she asked gently.

"I'll bet he walked the whole way to heaven."

❧❧❧

Just as my father's illness set a whirlwind of chaotic action in motion, so did his death. I had gone to Chicago to present a writer's workshop and attend a few meetings. By the time my sister called to tell me that our father had died, it was too late to cancel the workshop, so I fulfilled my obligation Monday evening, canceled the meetings scheduled for the rest of the week and flew back to Pennsylvania the next day. Once I arrived, there was not a moment of downtime. From retrieving out-of-town relatives at the airport to selecting hymns, readings and flowers to finding space to accommodate the avalanche of food sent by friends, we were all left feeling more numb than grief-stricken. The day immediately after the funeral, I had to drive twelve hours back to Atlanta with Dick and Torrie (who had driven up for the funeral) so that I could be in class Monday morning to administer mid-term exams. I could not miss any more work.

For the next five weeks my life was consumed with teaching, both days and evenings, trying to handle my father's affairs long distance, frequent phone consultations about Torrie's college love life (yes, break up with him, I was never crazy about him and, let's be honest here, he has dumb-looking hair), as well as trying to decipher (and withstand) Dick's increasingly difficult and hurtful behavior. Throughout the 23 years of our relationship I had certainly been on the receiving end of his frequent prickly moods and lengthy periods of withdrawal, but this was a different animal. He had passed his usual setting of "cold" weeks back and had quickly advanced to "cruel." As it turned out, his initial response to my father's diagnosis (the annoyed "Oh, God") was the high point of his sympathy and support during my dad's illness, death and aftermath. Dick never once, not one single time, spoke to my father the entire two-and-a-half months that he lay dying. Not one time. Even when I asked him to, or maybe especially when I asked him to. Months later, after we had separated, I asked him point blank why he had refused to call my father. He explained with a casual shrug that "it just wasn't a priority" for him. Oh. Good to know. I would like to point out, however, that it *was* a priority for him to call my father shortly before his diagnosis and ask for $25,000 to shore up his secretly sinking business venture. Excuse me, to be completely accurate, and to tell you all you need to know about the character of each man, Dick asked for $10,000 and my dad, without hesitation, gave him $25,000.

And so, as soon as my classroom door was locked for summer

break, I loaded my dog and myself into my car and headed back to Pennsylvania to sort out my father's affairs and shore up my mother. A week into the process, I realized how naive I had been with my original timeframe of completing everything in "a week or so." Make no mistake: the business of life isn't easy, but the business of death is enough to kill you. Good grief, the documentation merry-go-round does not stop. You go from attorney to accountant to insurance broker and back around, again and again. You need to locate and produce— in the original Greek if possible, and in triplicate at minimum—insurance policies, tax forms, death certificates, car titles, bank statements, house deeds and *my dad's honorable discharge papers from the Navy...from 1945, for crying out loud!* Oh, yeah, not a problem, I have those right here at my fingertips...you know, right next to my box of radio vacuum tubes and my collection of Andrews Sisters 78s!

That was all in addition to tending to the day-to-day activities of running a household, most of which had been neglected since my father had gotten sick three months earlier. I was facing a stack of monthly bills to pay, quarterly taxes to file (and I wasn't sure for which quarter) and a mountain of newspapers to recycle, not to mention a refrigerator of expired food, a leaning mailbox with a broken hinge and a car with an annual inspection sticker two days from expiration. I had barely stopped long enough to drink a large diet Coke all week, yet I hadn't made a dent in all that needed to be done.

In my defense, my progress had been severely hampered by a factor beyond my control. Namely, my dad. He, a first class specimen of no-nonsense, left-brained organization and order, had left much of his estate in uncharacteristic and quite astonishing disarray. Certainly, no one—least of all my dad himself—had been prepared for his very sudden passing, so some loose ends were to be expected. Loose ends, ha! More like skeins of unraveled strands cascading from every file folder I opened, burying me under an avalanche of loose ends. This was so much more than I had bargained for. Now I realize no one likes to plan for his own demise—although, at 82, you would think there might be *some* sense of urgency—but this mish-mashed mess had to put my dad in a class by himself. I was beginning to see that his denial of death, which had seemed such a blessing before, came with a cost, as I was neck-deep in the fallout of it. I felt like I needed a hazmat team and I didn't even have a pair of rubber gloves.

I decided to tackle the finances first. I followed the paper trail as best I could, from unidentified account numbers written on the back of an envelope to random notes about a few stocks scribbled in the margins of calendars to mysterious markings on a napkin from The Taproom at Mountain View Inn. I was terrified to throw away any gum wrapper or straw paper I found on the floor without thoroughly checking it for some cryptic message. All of these incoherent bits and pieces of information coexisted alongside legitimate documents and statements stuffed within a filing system that can only be described as unique. For example, my dad's stockbroker (make that *one* of my dad's stockbrokers—turns out he had five) directed me to look for a particular AT&T stock certificate. I took a remote chance on logic and looked under "A." Nothing. I tried "T" for "telephone company." I even tried "P" for phone." Nothing. So, I started going through the alphabet letter by letter and found the damn thing filed under "H." H? For what? For "Hell, I don't know where to put this" or for "Here it is"? Who knows?

How could this be the work of my dad, a man who could do ten pages of trigonometry calculations longhand and not misplace a single decimal point? Now, here I was trying to find a hypotenuse in a haystack. It seemed almost as if my dad had deliberately devised a system no one but he could understand as his insurance against death. If the grim reaper ever came knocking for him, my dad could simply point to this filing system and explain he couldn't go as there was no one else on earth who could understand it. Unfortunately, for all of us who loved him so much, his plan had failed and Daddy was now truly gone. I stopped by his grave several times to keep him apprised of my progress, and I usually ended my visit by joking with him that if he weren't already dead, I would kill him for leaving me with this mess!

While taking care of business was critical, I was also keeping a very close watch on my mother who seemed to be deteriorating before my eyes. My mother has never looked or acted her age, and at 84 she enjoyed excellent health and independence. She had borne up beautifully throughout my father's illness, driving herself back and forth to the hospital and nursing home every day, taking care of all the day-to-day details of his care on her own. She oversaw all the funeral arrangements with great calm and care, and though her personality leaned to the high-strung, emotional side (as do the personalities of all the women in my family!), she was perfectly composed from the funeral home to the church to the cemetery.

When I had first arrived on this trip, she was up and about and we had even gone to church and out to lunch. But as the days went on, she had started spending more and more time in bed. Each time I peeked into her room, she was asleep, curled into a tight ball with her arms covering her head, as if to prevent the painful reality of my dad's death from penetrating her. It was heartrending to see.

By week's end, when she was sleeping almost 24 hours a day, waking only to adamantly refuse to eat or drink anything, I was concerned. When she became difficult to rouse, I was concerned and scared. I called her doctor, who, via a nurse's message, quickly dismissed my mother's behavior as "quite normal" after suffering a personal loss. "Quite normal," really? When I had to physically shake her awake the next day and she was confused, and too weak and dizzy to stand, I was concerned, scared and angry. I called the doctor back to state emphatically that in my humble layperson's opinion this did not seem "quite normal" at all. When my mother's doctor had not returned my call as promised after five hours, I called back. The nurse told me the doctor would not be able to call me back that day...and then she whispered conspiratorially, "Take your mom to the ER right now. It will be two days before you hear back from the doctor."

After expressing my incredulity, I told her that we were already on the way and thanked her for being honest with me.

She replied, "You didn't hear it from me, okay?"

My mother, her sodium levels having plummeted to the danger zone, spent three days in the hospital having fluids pumped into her. But, gee, apparently, that's all "quite normal" after suffering a personal loss.

My stay in Pennsylvania—which I had first predicted would take no longer than ten days—took every day of the month of June, my entire summer break. I needed to go back to work, so I left my refueled mother with strict care instructions and a promise to return for a long weekend to check on everything in July. When I returned at the end of July, things were progressing well.

And that brings us back around to August 13 and my "Been-to-Canaan" meltdown. I understand now the song had little to do with my dad directly, and everything to do with me. The purity of Carole King's voice sliced through me with a fierce and unexpected potency, leaving every nerve in my body feeling exposed and raw. Every emotion that the responsibilities of the past several months had insulated me against came flooding out from what felt like the very marrow of my soul. And once the dam had broken, there was no obligation—including having to teach a class that morning with a modicum of composure—strong enough to stifle the intense torrent of hurt and anger and fear that had been unleashed. Through choking sobs of jagged-edged grief, I begged the heavens to let me go back to Canaan… back to that idyllic yestertime…when I believed life was secure and the world welcoming…when I greeted every day with the confident expectation born of innocence…when I could hear the screen door bouncing shut as my dad left for his Saturday golf game…my mother and aunt at the kitchen table gossiping in Piemontese, so "little pitchers with big ears" couldn't understand…the crunch of the gravel under the tires of my boyfriend's car, pulling up to my house…back to when all of my loved ones were here and healthy and whole. In Canaan my friend Kim was still a majorette, not a cancer statistic, my friend Ginny talked to her mother and sister at home where they belonged, not at the cemetery, and my sister Rosalie was still vibrant and strong, not crippled by the cruel ravages of Parkinson's disease. Oh, how desperately I wanted to go back to the sweet days of Canaan. At that moment I couldn't think of anything I wanted more, but my cries and pleas heavenward were met only with silence, affirming the answer I already knew: the dominant movement of life is forward, and we must all move on. I understood that I had no choice but to move on, but, in that moment, I also understood that, ironically, sometimes going backward a bit is what allows us to ultimately go forward. Taking a day trip to Canaan every now and then—if only in my mind—is what has helped me move past the awful pain of my father's death and has allowed me to begin enjoying his memory.

And I think knowing that would put a smile on my father's face. I can pretty much imagine his response to my long, convoluted story.

"So, you're okay now, Shorty?" he'd ask, heading efficiently to the bottom line. "Well, it does my heart good to hear that," he'd add, satisfied that that was all he really needed to know.

Of course, to himself he'd probably characterize all my carrying on about Canaan and crying and Carole King as a lot of extra "hooey." And that would put a smile on *my* face because I'd expect no less of him.

Rest in peace, Daddy. I love you. And be assured, *that* is no hooey!

3

Working at the Car Wash Blues

IF YOU WERE around during the 70s, (and by 70s, I mean the 1970s, not your own personal age), you may recognize this chapter's title as the name of an old Jim Croce song. I don't think it was ever released as a single, but I clearly remember it as the last song on the first side of the *Photographs and Memories* album, a record I very nearly wore out as the soundtrack to my life in 1974. The song's lyrics are humorously self-mocking and tell the tale of a self-recognized genius who, unable to convince anyone else of his superiority, is forced to labor at the carwash. By the chorus it's clear that the guy has a serious case of the car wash blues. I'm sure I absentmindedly hummed along many times—perhaps even blithely sang the words aloud—without having a clue about the true and tragic lot of the carwash worker. Boy, I know now it's not all glamour, and from the other side of enlightenment, I want to offer a belated, but heartfelt, coda of "Amen, brother."

If it's true, as Shakespeare more or less said, that some are born great car washers, some achieve car washing greatness, and others have car washing greatness thrust upon them, then I was certainly among the thrust-upon group, although I am not so deluded as to consider myself great. My short-lived car wash career began with the very best, most selfless intentions towards my dog and ended two hours later with my proclaiming loudly and repeatedly a term that would seem to be a rather obvious assessment of said male dog—son of a …! How had my good intentions deteriorated so completely?

It was a hot and extraordinarily sticky Sunday afternoon in Pennsylvania. I had gone there to help my mother with everything that needed to be done after my father's death. The air that particular Sunday was saturated with moisture and seemed almost too thick and heavy to breathe. Dry sponges swelled to capacity just sitting out in the open and my hair was pumped up to the size of the Iberian Peninsula. It had broken free of every single restraining device I had used all day to contain it. I have more hair than all of France, hair thick enough to shelter small birds, hair that may still contain a bobby pin or two from the updo I wore to my senior prom. Add 1000% humidity to the picture and we are talking about a force of nature, a weapon of mass destruction. Barrettes pop, scrunchies snap and "chopsticks" shoot through the air like missiles when my hair decides to flex its muscle. I had been locked in battle with it all day up in my parents' very un-airconditioned attic as I sorted through a lifetime accumulation of belongings among the cobwebs and creepy crawlers.

I was hot, sweaty, itchy, irritable and ready to tear my hair out by its Sequoia-sized roots after it broke free for the third time in an hour. That was it, I decided. I had had enough for one day and I went downstairs to cool off. I plopped myself down on the couch in the family room, directly in line with the stream of cool air flowing from the a/c vent. My skin was so soaked with perspiration, I couldn't stand to have any part of my body make contact with any other part. It was a challenge to keep my midlife thighs from spreading toward each other like cake batter in a warm oven, but I finally maneuvered myself into a fairly comfortable, if visually unflattering, position—arms and legs splayed, a/c hitting me dead-on and an icy cold diet Coke in hand.

"Ahhhhh," I sighed aloud. I think it was the first true break I'd had in a week. Just then I heard an even louder "Ahhhhh." It was my dog Jif exhaling as he slowly sank down against the wall and belly-flopped the final few inches to the floor. Unlike mine, his heavy sigh had the distinct sound of boredom, not relief. Oh, shoot, I thought, as a small twinge of guilt registered. My poor dog had been cooped up all week with no one to play with and very little attention from me. His big excitement for the past seven days had consisted of seeking out cool, uncarpeted floor surfaces to stretch out on.

"But, geez, I just now got comfortable," I protested aloud. Another heavy (melodramatic? martyr-like?) dog sigh. Oh, man, couldn't I just pretend I hadn't heard him? The last thing on earth I felt like doing was going out in the late afternoon heat and humidity for a rousing round of fetch...especially since I often ended up doing all the fetching as Jif, ADHD poster dog, was distracted from his mission by every microscopic gnat that buzzed by. He sighed again and I made the fatal flaw of looking his way and establishing eye contact. Caramel-brown, pathetic puppy-dog eyes beseeched me. I swear he was actually tearing up and his lower "lip" was quivering. Good grief, at only 3½ in human years, he was more adept at inducing guilt with just a look than most mothers twice his age in dog years.

"Okay, c'mon, Jif, let's go," I said with resignation. My sigh of defeat was completely drowned out by his yips of joy. He was on his feet and at the door in a nanosecond. He was positively dancing with excitement, his little doggy behind twitching faster than if he'd backed into a colony of fire ants. I corralled him long enough to put on his leash, and out the door we went. One step out the front door and—*slam*—I crashed into what seemed like an impenetrable wall of heat. The combination of the stifling heat, Jif's energy level of 25 on a scale of 1 to 10 and his complete inability to walk more than two feet in a straight line when on a leash—despite $500 spent on a private so-called trainer—forced me to consider an alternative to walking him for any distance.

"What we need," I said to Jif, "is some activity that will completely wear you out without in any way disrupting my state of lethargy." I tried to think of a suitable active dog/passive owner activity. I had a sudden thought, but then dismissed it, figuring June wasn't the best time to train him to haul me around town on the old sled hanging in the garage. The metal runners scraping against the pavement would make a horrible racket. Man, where was a rickshaw when you needed one? That would have been the ticket. Hitch Jif up and off we'd go. By the time he finished lugging my slothful self around the block a few times, he'd be reduced to a limp, wet furball and I would not have expended a single calorie.

Then it hit me, what seemed an inspired idea. I would drive Jif over to the high school, my alma mater, where he could run free and I could sit motionless on a bench and finish my diet Coke. The school is located in a rural area outside of town, set back far from the road, on property completely buffered by fields on one side and a farm on the other. I could still remember watching the sheep migrate across the hillside at exactly 10 o'clock every day during Miss Cunningham's English class. Once the sheep were on the move, I knew I only had 20 minutes left to distinguish the participles from the gerunds on my worksheet. On another hillside field, visible from my geometry class, the cows were the timekeepers. Geometry was my last class of the day, and I could count down my final minutes of captivity by monitoring the cows' position. At the start of class, they were high on the hill. As the class progressed, they moseyed down the hillside toward the school. When they reached ground level, their heads perfectly framed by the classroom windows, I knew I was in the home stretch. Oh, what a welcome sight those cows' heads were. They were there to liberate me. Harbingers of blessed freedom, guardians of the sacred extracurricular time, cows were my heroes.

All of which made the betrayal I came to suffer at their hands—well, hooves—even more painful. Jif bounded from the car the instant I opened the back door and then he stopped dead in his tracks. He was visibly overwhelmed at the prospect of claiming such wide-open space as his own. He stood for a moment, almost quaking in disbelief at his good fortune. Then he took off. And he did not stop for a long time. He ran full tilt, back and forth, in straight lines, zigzags and circles, across the large parking lot, through one field, then another and back around again. And all the while, I just sat and sipped. I was just about to reach around to pat myself on the back for having had the brilliant idea of bringing Jif here, when he suddenly came to a screeching halt in the middle of the parking lot and cocked his head as if he'd heard one of those silent dog whistles. He stood completely still, except for his twitching nose, which sniffed at the air furiously, as if deciphering some Morse code message carried on the wind. And then it happened. He deciphered the encrypted message, which apparently directed him to run at top speed across the entire parking lot all the way to the other side of the school building— straight to the hillside cow pasture. Judging by his speed and single-mindedness, the message effectively conveyed the irresistible allure of the cow pasture, with its promises of sights he'd never seen and smells he'd never smelled…not to mention, things to roll in that he'd never rolled in.

I hadn't thought that far ahead yet, though. Initially, I was only worried about him getting kicked or butted. I had a horrible vision of spooked cows going berserk and Jif being too fascinated or too dumb to get out of harm's way. He clearly had no such concerns as he was gone in a flash, with me trailing in his wake, screaming in vain for him to come back. Well, I thought with some relief, as I tore across the parking lot, the pasture was fenced, so he wouldn't be able to do more than poke his nose through the wires. That surely wouldn't set off a stampede, I hoped. I reached the hillside just in time to see him find the only hole in the entire length of the wire fence and wriggle his disobedient, despicable and completely delighted self through it into the pasture.

The only good news was that there were no cows in the pasture (no geometry classes to keep track of in summer), so the stampede risk was eliminated. The cows, however, had left several calling cards behind. This had to be the richest soil west of the Fertile Crescent. Jif was definitely in deep—shoulder-deep, to be specific—doo-doo. You know the old, rather crass, expression about being as happy as a pig in —? Well, let me tell you, a pig may stop at happy, but Jif was completely ecstatic. He ran and skidded, tumbled and rolled, sporting a big, dopey dog grin the whole time. The stuff clung to his fur in clumps, chunks and lumps. The more he cavorted around, the more thickly and thoroughly he was covered. He looked like a giant Dilly Bar from Dairy Queen…with a more distinctive aroma.

I, of course, was hysterical, fearing that if he headed over the hill into the nether reaches of the farm I would lose him forever. I knew I had to get him to come out the way he went in, but had no idea how to do that or what on earth I would do with him afterwards. At first I ran back and forth in front of the fence, whooping and hollering like a lunatic, trying to make myself, as the "trainer" had instructed, more interesting to him than what currently held his attention. It's pretty humbling when you have to consciously work at being more interesting than cow poop. She had said a runaway dog would only come to you if you seemed to be more fun than his other options. I flapped my arms frantically and made every weird high- and low-pitched noise I was capable of, but he all he did was run happily back and forth on the other side of the fence. He thought it was a wonderful game. And then I remembered the trainer also saying that dogs interpret your trying to catch them as a game of "chase," and that if you wanted the dog to come to you, you had to run in the opposite direction so he would follow. I had been afraid to run away from the fence and lose sight of him, but I was desperate enough by then to try almost anything.

"Okay, Jif," I yelled, "I'm leaving, bye-bye."

I started toward the parking lot and my car. It worked…too well. Jif really took that "bye-bye" to heart and started racing toward the pasture fence to come with me. The problem was he couldn't find the opening and he started to panic. He started digging at the ground in a mad frenzy to open another escape route. That, of course, only served to stir up more, er, crap, which flew up in the air and landed on him—once, right in the middle of his head. I had to laugh in spite of the circumstances. I ran back up to the fence and tried to steer him to the opening with verbal commands, but he was long past reasoning and only continued his panicked digging, rolling and skidding along his side of the fence. It was a nightmare, and the longer it went on, the closer I came to tears. It had all just been too, too much, this day, this week, this whole stinking–literally, now–year. I just stood there, crying helplessly.

"It's all too hard," I sobbed to no one, as I sank down on the grass. "I can't fix any of the things that have gone so terribly wrong. I can't do it. I cannot do it. I give up," I wailed at the heavens. I was prepared to just sit there in the grass like that until I died, shriveled up and blew away.

God must have finally taken pity on me because all of a sudden, Jif shot past me, as if violently spewed from the mouth of the beast. He made a bee line for the car and didn't stop until he got there. He stood panting at the door, waiting for me to come let him in. I ran down to the car and my momentary relief evaporated as I faced the reality of the situation. I was stuck alone, in the middle of a secluded parking lot, with a 70-pound dog, covered in 50 pounds of cow manure on a beastly hot afternoon, with no means of transporting him out of there except via the buff leather interior of my car. I wanted to die. I also wanted a gas mask. But since neither desire was likely to be fulfilled right then, I had to come up with a solution, and fast, because Jif's new coat was curing quickly in the heat. If it petrified, I thought, I'd need a jackhammer to get it off him.

"Okay," I said to myself, "first things first." I had to secure Jif in case the effectiveness of threatening to leave him wore off and he decided to bolt again. Holding my nose, as well as Jif at as long an arm's length as possible, I carefully hooked his leash to his collar. I tramped on the other end with my foot so that I had both my arms free. I remembered that in the trunk I had the seat cover I had used on the trip to Pennsylvania to keep Jif's nails from scratching up the upholstery. I got out the cover and arranged it as securely as I could over the back seat. My original plan was to drive Jif back to my parents' house and hose off the first several layers before moving in for the deep cleaning and disinfecting (in heavy-duty rubber gloves). I started mentally rehearsing my moves and ran headlong into some serious obstacles. When I pictured myself using the hose, I realized that with my dad no longer around tending his flowers, the hose was likely not even hooked up outside. It was probably in the basement, and I knew couldn't lift that heavy hose caddy and carry it up the outside steps by myself. My incapacitated mother would not be able to help me carry it or hold the dog or even gather the bucket, scrub brushes and gloves. She could barely respond to her name right now, so I'd definitely be on my own. What to do? I needed to find a place with an accessible hose, water and soap, some place that wouldn't be destroyed by my cleaning mission. It was then that I had a sudden flash of genius (or insanity) and, bereft of any better options, decided on the spot to go with it.

"All right, let's do this thing," I said to Jif decisively. Still holding my nose, I opened the back car door and he leapt onto the covered seat. I got behind the wheel, opened all the windows and sped off down the road, less than a mile to my destination: an old-fashioned, do-it-yourself car wash. Yes, I said car wash. Okay, so maybe the idea leaned more to insanity than genius, but I was out of aces. In my defense, I must point out that, in theory, this was an inspired idea. It met all of the criteria—water source, hose, soap, all contained in a virtually indestructible facility, with floor drains even. It was perfect. I pulled into the parking lot feeling pretty proud of myself.

Once again, let me say that *in theory* this was an inspired idea. In this particular instance, however, theory fell very short. Theory over-looked some critical real-life variables, such as 1) Jif's outsized fear of unfamiliar spaces—cow pastures apparently being the exception—as well as all unfamiliar noises, people, vehicles, furniture, wallpaper, jewelry, neckties, freckles, hairstyles, ringtones, well, you get the idea. I don't mean he was skittish. I mean he came positively *unhinged* in the face of any unknown element, straining and pulling violently on his leash to escape the danger posed by an unfamiliar baseball cap or briefcase (again, unfamiliar cow poop being a notable excep-tion). At such times, a supernatural strength possessed him, and if you happened to be attached to the other end of his leash, you had no choice but to go along for the ride. If he were not on a leash, there was a chance you might never see him again, so thoroughly could fear motivate him. He would not, *could not*, be soothed or calmed by any means. His default setting was "run furiously in the opposite direction" until reaching what he felt was a safe harbor, possibly in another zip code.

2) Of all the threats to Jif's safety and well-being, he perceived none greater than that posed by a fishing rod. I had personally witnessed him shoot like a rocket from lake's edge to the summit of a half-mile hill in two seconds flat upon spying a lone fishing pole being toted on a trail 1,000 yards away.

3) To a fear-crazed, manure-covered dog, the soap & water dispensing "wand" at a car wash looks a lot like a fishing pole.

Jif put the brakes on the second I opened the back door of the car. One quick glance around the parking lot was sufficient for him to determine that he was having no part in this fool's errand. This place barked DANGER to him, fraught as it was with such menacing elements as a large, rusty trash barrel and an old, beat-up Coke machine. Not to mention the mysterious cement block structure leering at him from across the lot. Why, every way he turned, it was chock full of the unfamiliar! I knew that achieving my purpose here would not be easy, but I was resolute. I choked up on the leash as far as my olfactory nerves would allow and yanked as hard as I could, trying to budge him from the back seat. After several attempts, I finally dislodged him onto the pavement, along with the seat cover and two loose nuggets of manure. I dragged him across the parking lot against the strong resistance of all four of his legs in "park." I was dripping with perspiration, gasping for air and my hands were cramping painfully from holding the leash so tightly, but I didn't give in. He strained mightily with his head and shoulders to pull me in the opposite direction, but I strained more mightily to pull him to the first empty car-washing stall. I was *not* losing this one! I grunted and groaned louder than a Sumo wrestler with a hernia and finally wrangled the obstinate beast into the stall. I felt a rush of victory, which turned out to be short-lived.

For starters, I had accomplished the impossible, not by muscling Jif inside the stall, but by finding the one spot outside of hell during the rainy season that was even more miserably hot and humid than the great outdoors this day. The cement blocks, sun-baked on the outside and water-drenched on the inside, made for a steam room that rivaled that of the most exclusive health spa. The walls were incredibly effective at trapping odors as well—and I can't adequately describe the smell captured in that space once Jif and the hot steam made contact. Choking back bile and straining to see through the haze, I assessed the situation and realized that "good, old-fashioned" wasn't always so good. This was a bare bones operation that had undergone precious little updating since it had opened at least 35 years before. Old-fashioned here meant the hose or wand was coin-operated, dispensing soap and water at the rate of 75 cents for three minutes—payable in quarters only. There would be no new-fangled ATM swiping here, no prepaying for a code, not so much as a "good, old-fashioned" change machine. I had shoved some money—and my now useless ATM card—in my pocket before getting out of the car. I pulled the money out of my pocket to find I had three quarters among the worthless nickels, dimes and bills. It would only buy me three minutes, but it was a start, I thought. Maybe I could scrounge up a few more quarters in the car after I got the first coat of crud off Jif.

I fed the three quarters into the slot and picked up the wand. Jif, who had not calmed down one iota, very nearly lost his mind when he saw me coming at him with a "fishing pole," spraying a sudsy mix. Trying to hold onto a madly squirming dog with one hand and wield the *un*wieldy wand with the other was a near-impossible feat. I pulled the trigger, but couldn't hit my target for anything, instead spraying the walls, the floor and myself, right in the face. The soapy water stung my eyes and I squeezed them shut, with my finger still on the trigger of the wand. I blindly fired off round after round of soapy spray and eventually managed to blast Jif broadside. That's when the sh-- really hit the fan, so to speak. The water pressure knocked a few chunks of Jif's manure armor loose and catapulted them through the air, one narrowly missing my head. They hit the floor and fairly exploded upon impact, scattering myriad, but still potent, splinters into every nook and cranny. The shock of the blast sent Jif into panic over-drive and he jerked hard on the leash. The soapy spray had made the floor more slippery than an ice rink and when Jif jerked, I could no longer hold my ground. I went scooting along the slick concrete, my feet slipping and sliding every which way in my soggy sandals until I completely lost my balance and crash-landed flat on my behind in the middle of the sopping wet concrete floor. With the jolt of the fall, my barrette popped open, sending a dripping mop of coils cascading into my face and down my back. Meanwhile, my tailbone felt like it had shattered when it hit the floor just as surely as the flying manure chunks had. The pain was searing and for several stunned seconds I couldn't move. I just sat there on the swampy, poop-strewn floor, the dirty water seeping through my shorts to my underwear. The wand, which I had dropped when I fell, jammed in the "on" position and continued to spray plumes of foamy water, which shot up in the air and showered back down on me. Jif huddled in a corner, quivering and hyperventilating. Talk about your carwash blues. This was no way to make a living.

And it was then, at that moment when I was contemplating death for myself and/or my dog for about the fifth time that day, that I felt it. It started as a kind of gurgling from deep inside of me and gathered strength as it forced its way up from my bowels, through my stomach, up my throat and out of my mouth. I parted my lips and out came this primal kind of guttural growl, "Son of a biiiitch!" I roared.

I'm not sure, but I believe I roared it, uh, several times in succession. It felt like—and must have sounded like—an exorcism. Even Jif stopped quivering and stood completely still. Then he sat down—*sat down*, I say, *in the unfamiliar place*—and waited for a command from me. I felt a sudden sense of power over my circumstances. I rose to my feet just as a head (having heard the exorcism, no doubt) popped around the wall from the stall next door. The head, which belonged to a kid about 16, started to ask if I was okay, but stopped mid-sentence when he saw me in my condition…and Jif in his con-dition…and *no car* in any condition. I decided to act as if this were a perfectly normal situation.

"I'm fine, but I just realized I don't have any more quarters. Do you happen to have change for a dollar or two?" I asked. I pulled out the soaking wet bills from my soaking wet pocket and extended my soaking wet hand in the kid's direction.

"Uh, um, yeah, sure," he said hesitantly. I can only imagine that he had heard you had a better chance of surviving an encounter with a homicidal maniac if you played along with him, or in this case, her.

Well, he turned out to be a really nice kid who sympathized with me after hearing of Jif's and my escapades. He gave me enough quarters to finish washing Jif well enough to take him home and even gave me two old towels to dry him off (which he *insisted* I not return!). I even had enough change left over to get a diet Coke out of the ancient drink machine. As I pulled out of the parking lot with a damp, but less aromatic, dog in tow, I tuned the car radio to an oldies station. I'd love to say that "Working at the Car Wash Blues" came on—how perfect—but I don't believe that song ever received any airplay even in the 70s. I did hear quite a few of my old favorites, though, and had great fun singing along. And maybe it was better that way. After all, life seldom, if ever, gives us perfect. And often what appears perfect at first glance (like my "inspired" ideas) doesn't really measure up in the end. What life does seem to give us, however, is a fair share of what we need to keep singing along. True, I thought to myself, the notes had certainly seemed few and far between lately, but if I were honest, I had to admit that I'd managed to string together enough to sing a chorus or two, even in the darkest times. Driving home, listening to the oldies, I decided I'd just have to trust that, in time, I'd be given enough notes to write a whole new song for my life. Grace notes, I thought fittingly, and I made a conscious decision to trust my life to grace. Feeling a slight sense of peace for the first time that day, I tossed back the last of my diet Coke and turned up the radio. Yes, I would trust in grace all right, but, just to be on the safe side, I would also carry a roll of quarters in my car at all times!

4

The View From Down Here: Time out of Mind on April 7, 2003

WHO ARE YOU? I struggled to assemble even this simple thought as, stunned, I looked up at Dick's profile, silhouetted by the car's light against the night sky. I was splayed awkwardly on the asphalt surface of the street in front of our house. Leaning on one elbow, my right leg twisted painfully under me, I instinctively reached out for the hand that had held mine for the past 23 years, but which, incomprehensibly, had just seconds ago pushed me down onto the ground. Confusion and disbelief. The whole incident had happened so quickly, I couldn't quite process it. My brain was swimming, drowning, in a sea of sensations and half-formed thoughts. It seemed so unreal, as if it were taking place in a dream. Maybe it hadn't really happened at all. Had it? Yes, it had. The burning scrapes on my knee, ankle and elbow attested to it. As did my left sandal, which had flown off my foot when I hit the ground and now lay on its side a few yards away from me.

Dazed and disheveled, I looked to Dick for an explanation to set things right, to make sense out of this chaos. I fully expected him to explain that it had been an accident and that he certainly had not meant to knock me down. I expected him to help me up, apologize for having accidentally pushed me off balance and possibly even realize in that horrible moment that he was out of control in many ways.

Instead, he looked down at me disgustedly, with his hands on his hips, and sneered, "Get up."

"Wh-what?" I asked, as if he were speaking a language that I couldn't understand.

"Get up," he repeated, with undisguised scorn.

I felt as if I were submerged in quicksand, unable to move.

"Get up. What's your problem?" he repeated, less sympathetically than before, if that were even possible.

"What's my problem?" I cried, my voice cracking. "My God, Dick, you actually knocked me down on the ground."

"You...fell," he said coldly, looking straight ahead through narrowed eyes.

"Okay, yes, I fell—because you pushed me," I said.

"Just get up and get out of my way," he said as he got in the driver's seat of his car. I scrambled to my feet, unaided, and brushed myself off. My favorite black skirt was now torn. He slammed the car door shut and drove off without looking back. I watched his car leave the neighborhood and asked again, aloud this time, who he was. Who? Someone I no longer knew. Someone I didn't care to know, yet someone who would, over the next few years, slash and burn a wide path through my life, leaving little but scorched earth behind.

How in the world had my life come to this?

❧❧❧❧

Back to the Beginning: December 22, 2002, Shock and Awfulness Unleashed

The precipitating event that led to me finding myself on the ground on the evening of April 7, 2003, had taken place a few months earlier. Shock and awfulness was set in motion around 6:00 in the evening on December 22, 2002, the Sunday before Christmas. I was running very much behind my usual schedule for getting into the Christmas spirit. Most years I would have hosted two parties by this time and would have been putting the finishing touches on the seating chart for Christmas dinner. But this was not most years. This was year my father had died and the year my mother had nearly died, twice. It turned out that my mother's episode of electrolyte imbalance that had landed her in the hospital for three days in June was a mild precursor of what was to come. Despite holding steady through the summer, she apparently fell off the cliff of grief about the beginning of September when she stopped eating altogether, got in bed and never got out. By the third week of September, her disjointed speech on the phone told me something was seriously amiss and I flew up to Pennsylvania to retrieve her. She was barely 80 pounds, combative and delirious, the result of her sodium level plummeting after weeks of virtual starvation. Within hours of being admitted to the hospital here in Atlanta, she was a breath away from having a brain seizure. The doctors explained to me that as dangerously low as her sodium level was, it was even more dangerous to raise it too quickly, and as a result she would likely deteriorate even more before she would get better. If indeed she would get better, they added, as it was possible she wouldn't survive. It was a harrowing three weeks, during which time she fell into a semi-conscious state, her eyes shut tight as she mumbled and thrashed around for several days. It was so frightening and heartbreaking to see her like that—hooked up to monitors and IV's, in a diaper and restraints, grunting and groaning madly for hours on end. When at last she opened her eyes and started to interact, she had no idea of her surroundings or who anyone was. When she was finally physically strong enough to be discharged from the hospital, she was transferred to a geriatric psychiatric facility where she spent an additional two weeks being evaluated for long-term cognitive effects. She had been discharged shortly before Thanksgiving and had moved in with my sister in Florida where she was continuing to make progress in her recovery.

How, I wondered, cutting vegetables at the kitchen counter, could it have been only twelve months since my parents had been in this very house, celebrating Christmas with my family, my in-laws and assorted friends, with none of us having any hint of the profound changes in the offing. How could we have sat right next to my father those two weeks and never detected a single clue of the cancer that was viciously devouring him from the inside out? What a cowardly enemy cancer is, going about its destruction in quiet darkness. I was struggling to keep these thoughts from overtaking me as I went about preparing a special dinner for Torrie, who would soon be arriving home from college with her new boyfriend in tow. For her sake, I had forced myself to put on a happy face and play catch up with decking the halls. I suddenly remembered that I had run out of hooks for the last few ornaments and had not made it to the store that afternoon to get more. I couldn't leave the house then in the middle of cooking dinner, so I walked into the living room to ask Dick to run to the store, so the tree would be "perfect" when the kids arrived. I found him sitting in the dark, slumped in an arm chair. At first glance, I thought he was just quietly admiring the lit Christmas tree. Just as I was about to ask him if he would run to the store, he looked over at me and blurted out, "I'm leaving."

"Oh, okay, are you going to Target? Because we need more hooks. I was just going to ask you to go," I replied.

"No, I'm *leaving*," he repeated with emphasis.

"Walmart? K-k-kro-ger?" I asked, my voice cracking.

"I'm leaving *you*, Lee."

I remember sitting down on the couch. I remember compulsively twisting and untwisting the ties of my apron. I remember being unable to speak or even comprehend anything he said after "leaving… *you*." I know he continued talking because his mouth was moving, and I'm sure he was saying actual words, horrible and scary words, but it all sounded like Charlie Brown's teacher to me. Actually, like Charlie Brown's teacher underwater. With me wearing ear muffs. Just an endless and muffled chorus of "Waa-waa-waaaa."

After several minutes, I came out of my aphasia enough to understand that he was spilling out details of an obviously well thought-out plan. This was not, he made clear in both substance and style, a negotiation; it was the handing down of an edict, a unilateral decision. He did not want to be married to me, he said. Not now, not ever, not even a little bit. There was no one else, nothing like that, he insisted, he just wanted out. And "going forward," as he said, it would work like this: He would stay through Christmas, during which time I was not to tell anyone, least of all Torrie, what was going on because he didn't want to spoil anyone's holidays or deal with anyone's reactions or questions. Apparently, he didn't consider me "anyone." I was to go through all the motions of Christmas dinner, present opening and family activities, including the three of us painting Torrie's new college apartment together, like one big happy family, appearances being critical, of course. He would spend the day before New Year's Eve with me, take me out to eat—to one of our favorite places, no less—and the next morning, New Year's Eve, he would get on a plane and fly to Arizona where he would spend a week hiking in the mountains, and where, he emphasized, there were no land line phones or cell phone reception. Then, he would return to Atlanta and move his things into an apartment he had already rented close to his office. As for the actual dissolution of the marriage, he said he'd probably have to "divorce me pretty quick" (his actual words) to keep his options open, but nothing was set in stone yet, so he'd have to get back to me on that one. And, bing, bang, boom, easy-peasy, there you had it. He had his whole new life planned out and I was still twisting my apron in my lap, wondering who was going to Target to buy the extra hooks we needed.

I felt like someone who had been unexpectedly overtaken by a surging tide, completely without footing, desperately grasping for a passing branch—a twig— to stop myself from being completely swept away. Dazed and disoriented, I tried to latch onto a word or two to help me regain my balance. Of the torrent of bewildering words rushing by me, "Arizona" struck me as particularly odd, and I snatched at it. Not that having my husband proclaim out of the blue, "Hey, I'm divorcing you and going hiking for a week" wasn't sufficiently odd in and of itself, but Arizona seemed as foreign and strange a destination to me as Venus. We lived nearly 2,000 miles from there, had never been there, knew no one who lived there and, as far as I knew, neither of us had ever in all of our years together expressed any desire to go there. I wasn't even sure if he knew it was a state.

"Arizona?" I sputtered. "That's ridiculous. Why are you going all the way to Arizona? That's just crazy." Yes, it's true, my husband had just announced the imminent dismantling of my entire life, of everything I knew and loved, and his odd choice for a hiking destination was all I objected to. Really? Gee, makes you wonder whether I would have found his plan acceptable if he'd said he was going to hop across the border to North Carolina instead. I think this narrow focusing must be some kind of coping mechanism, automatically triggered in the face of overwhelming and incomprehensible news. You cannot possibly take in the whole of it, so your mind picks out bits and pieces that seem to be in error, hoping, thereby, to expose the whole as flawed as well. It was as if I believed that pointing out the irrationality of his destination would render the whole plan unworkable. Surely, I remember thinking, we would both laugh about it in a few minutes and dismiss this whole episode as a kooky, passing fantasy, like wanting to join the circus or to run with the bulls.

Well, I was partially right—it was one supremely kooky plan, but it was not passing and it most certainly was not dismissed. He told me that his business partner, who had grown up years earlier in Arizona, had spoken of his home state with such fondness that he—Dick—just had to go and see for himself. That was all the explanation I ever got from him. He didn't say at the time whether anyone had also talked about abandoning his wife and daughter, with no intention of honoring any of his obligations, with such fondness that he'd had to try that out for himself, too.

I somehow stood up from the couch and began sleepwalking through the two weirdest weeks of my life, weeks that would have made a Dalí painting look pedestrian by comparison. Even more absurd than Dick's insistence that we carry out a charade of matrimonial bliss was his ability to execute it so superbly. He was a new and improved version of himself. He was actually nice. To *me*. Exceptionally so. Smiling, complimenting me, teasing me good-naturedly. It was bizarre, more than a little confusing, and in startling contrast to his actions and attitude towards me for at least the past year. Although never mistaken for jovial or high-spirited, in the past year his mood had registered at subterranean levels and his notorious passive-aggressive tendencies had morphed into frightening aggressive-aggressive ones. He was consistently short-tempered, nasty and distant. He missed no opportunity to snap at me and bullied me into back-pedaling and apologizing every time I dared question him over matters small—where are the scissors?—and large—where is all the money his new business was supposed to be generating?

Suddenly, having revealed his intention to leave me, he was the model husband. Geez, I thought, he should have decided to divorce me years ago, we would have had a much happier marriage! He hit his mark for every performance that week. On Christmas Day, in front of everyone, he made a great show of presenting me with an expensive painting by one of my favorite artists. The disparity between the apparent and the real pushed me to tears, at which point he whispered in my ear that he wanted me to have it for when he was gone. Like I was a runner-up on *Wheel of Fortune*, being sent home with the lovely parting gifts. I excused myself to the bathroom for a short cry and subsequent make-up repair because I couldn't break character! And it got stranger by the day. One evening Torrie asked us to have dinner at a restaurant where her boyfriend was waiting tables over Christmas vacation to make a few extra bucks. She thought it would be fun to surprise him and have him wait on us. That night, I swear we could have been on the cover of *Family Weekly* (if there is such a magazine). Dick was charm personified, throwing his arm around me playfully, patting my hand on the table and telling the boyfriend funny and flattering anecdotes about me. What the hell? I took another long rest room break.

Once Torrie returned to the town where she attended college 45 miles away, I was left alone with Dick while he prepared for his hiking adventure. That's when the weirdness reached a new level. He got out the suitcase and called me into the bedroom to help him decide what clothes to take.

"I don't know," I said to him, really not too concerned about the particular clothes he was wearing to apparently hike his way out of my life. "Hiking clothes, you know better than I do what to take for that." Was it really necessary to involve me in this?

"No, I mean, what do you think I should take for nice clothes?" he clarified.

"Why do you need nice clothes to hike in mountains so primitive there is no phone and so isolated there is no cell signal?" I asked, confused.

"Well, we spend the first night in Tucson. The camp's director picks us up in a van at the airport and takes us to a hotel. Then we are all going out to dinner to get to know each other a little before camping out together for a week," he explained, a little too smoothly, which I was too stupid and stunned to pick up on at the time.

For the next 45 minutes, I was treated to a fashion show of him in all manner of pants, shirts and sweater combinations, all of which highlighted his newly trimmed-down-by-fifty-pounds physique. I pronounced all of them to be fine choices as he preened and pranced in front of every mirror, checking himself from all angles. He selected four outfits to take.

"Why are you taking so many for one dinner?" I asked—and I'm amazed now that I had the presence of mind to at least question him on that point.

"Well, we spend the last night in Tucson, too, so I might need decent clothes for that, plus for flying back on the plane.

"Oh." I just let it go. I was too numb to feel and too tired to argue.

The next morning, at his insistence, he drove himself to the airport and pretty much flew out of my life. As he'd promised, I didn't hear a word from him for the next seven days. I mostly just lay on the bed crying off and on for the entire week and lying about it when anyone asked me what I had been doing. People have asked me how or why I went along with his cockamamie plan to carry on as if nothing had happened. A big part of the answer is that I was in shock and couldn't quite grasp, much less believe, that it was really happening. I think I hoped that it would all go away, like a bad dream. Dick's strategy of launching the attack almost as people were walking through the front door for Christmas also all but assured my compliance. Additionally, I knew how vindictive he could be when crossed, so I didn't think it was wise just then to add fuel to his already out-of-control fire.

On the evening Dick was supposed to return home, he didn't. Hour after hour passed with no sign of him. I never closed my eyes the whole night, calling his cell phone repeatedly, to no avail. When morning dawned, I still had not heard a word from him. I checked the news websites again and learned there had been no report of plane crashes between Tucson and Atlanta, which gave me little comfort because I simply switched the picture in my mind from him falling out of the sky to him falling off a mountain cliff instead. I was beside myself and felt helpless to do anything. I didn't even know precisely where he had gone, didn't know the name of the "mountain adventure" company, had no kind of emergency contact information at all, as he had refused to give me any details.

I had promised Torrie I would drive over to her college town that day and take her shopping to stock her new apartment's larder. I tried to keep my panic in check and decided not to say anything just yet. We were in Sam's Club, snapping up jarred spaghetti sauce when my in-laws called on Torrie's cell phone to see how her new year was going so far. When she handed me the phone, I tried to ask as nonchalantly as possible if they had happened to hear from their son, a question they rightly found odd, and which made Torrie's ears prick up. I did plenty of fast double-talking to make this situation sound as normal as possible, and if it sounded suspicious to them, they didn't question me about it, but expressed appropriate concern. As soon as Torrie hung up with her grandparents, her phone rang again. This time it was her boyfriend and the first thing she blurted out was, "We don't know where my dad is!" She was clearly upset and I tried to assure her that he and I had probably gotten our signals crossed and that he was likely coming home tonight instead of last night. That would explain his cell phone not working, I told her as support for my argument—he still hadn't descended from the mount back into civilization, thus no signal. I didn't believe a word of it, but I didn't know what I did believe either.

I drove home, wondering if I would be a widow before I would be a divorcee, finding both alternatives equally devastating. Before I went to bed that night, I tried Dick's cell phone one last time and, miracle of miracles, he actually answered. He told me he was on his way home from the airport, although he was short on both explanations and courtesy. He said only that he had missed his plane the day before and that he didn't owe me even that much explanation. Had I forgotten we were no longer a couple, he asked. Mr. Charming had obviously left not only the building, but the street, neighborhood and, I think, galaxy, as well. He never really returned. Torrie called right after I had hung up with her father, and it was clear from my voice that I had been crying. She asked me point blank what was going on. I told her a modified version, one I wanted very much to believe myself. I said that her father had been under a lot of stress with his fledgling business, working long hours, with the grueling Atlanta commute adding even more hours and tension to his long days, and that he felt he just needed some time alone to decompress and focus on the business. He would be living temporarily in an apartment a stone's throw from his business until he could get things under control. I tried to put as positive and non-catastrophic spin on it as I could, but she was still understandably upset. I said her father would talk to her when he got home. That turned out to be pretty much of a lie.

Dick's descent into insanity continued in earnest when he returned from his trip. First, he wanted me to go shopping with him for new things for his apartment, as if he were my son going off to college. When I declined, he actually accused me of not supporting him, historically one of his favorite tricks for manipulating me. And unlike every other instance before in our 22 years of marriage and one year of courtship, I had to admit that this time he was actually right—I really didn't support having "his" divorce foisted on me out of the blue. I knew, as he had made abundantly clear, that I could not stop him from doing whatever he wanted, but I certainly didn't have to go shopping with him, did I? Then he told me what furniture from our house he was taking to his new pad and asked me to pack up some household items for him to take as well. He told me he was making the big move Sunday morning with the help of a friend and a borrowed truck. He was practically walking on air, whistling while he worked, and full of excitement and anticipation on the eve of his new adventure. I, on the other hand, felt as if I'd been run over by the borrowed truck.

I had planned to leave the house very early on Sunday morning to go hear one of my students perform a solo at her church, a move I hoped would save me from witnessing the whole moving mess. I almost made it. I was just turning off the lights in my bedroom when I heard Dick's friend at the front door, a little earlier than anticipated. I really didn't feel like facing him, so I waited to slip out until I heard him going upstairs to retrieve a load of boxes. Again, my timing was off because as I was approaching the door, he came running down the stairs and we all but collided. I expected a quick, low-key kind of "hi" at most, but he greeted me with a hearty, "Hello, how's it going?" completely out of tune with his reason for being there. How's it going? Really? Had everyone lost their minds? This encounter so unnerved me that I practically jumped into my car to avoid further conversation…and promptly realized that in my haste and panic, I had left my purse inside the house. I went back in the house just in time to see Dick and his friend exchanging congratulatory high fives— "Way to go, dude!"—as they finished taping up some boxes. Talk about dancing on my grave. I fought back tears and nausea, grabbed my purse and sought asylum back in my car. I didn't care what else I may have forgotten—oxygen tank, prosthetic limb, artificial heart—I was not going back into that house again until I was sure Dick and his friend were gone.

The following couple of weeks brought revelation upon revelation, all unexpected and unwanted. I found out Dick had never paid

Torrie's tuition for the first semester of the year when she called in hysterics to say she had been barred from registering for the second semester; I found out he had never paid our property taxes when I received notice that our house was on the sheriff's auction list; I found out that he had not paid the utility bills for months when I came home to find my phone and power turned off. The list of unpaid and/ or past due notices was staggering and humiliating. I am the kind of person who cannot sleep if I owe anyone five cents, so my newly ac-quired debtor's status was particularly upsetting to me. I had handled the finances since the early years of our marriage when it had first become clear that Dick was not cut out for it. Little things like his buying a boat instead of paying the rent or buying a car without tell-ing me seemed to indicate that financial responsibility was not his strong suit. (Oddly enough, he managed million-dollar budgets at work with surgical precision.) We hadn't had a late payment or an unmet obligation since I had taken charge of the checkbook. I don't mean to imply that he did not work hard or could not make money; he did both well, but he couldn't hold onto money if it were super-glued to his palms. For the past year, though, he had taken back the reins of our day-to-day finances because 1) I had been out of town a lot due to my ailing parents and 2) according to him, our finances had become quite complicated since he had started his ill-conceived business venture and no longer got a regular paycheck. I was now beginning to face the extent of his mismanagement, which, tragically, reached far beyond unpaid bills.

Even though it had been clearly understood between us that dur-ing his tenure as our financial manager he was not to touch our long-term investments, retirement accounts, etc., without consulting me, I soon discovered that he had been moving that money around, fudg-ing numbers and outright lying to me about the business for the past year. His business was revealing itself to be little more than an elabo-rate shell game. I had been trying to pin him down on numbers for the past year, and he had evaded me at every turn. The day I came home to the gas company's big yellow "disconnected for nonpayment" tag on my front door, I called him at his office and demanded once again to know exactly what was going on and how we were going to divide assets in this divorce.

"Assets?" he snorted. "What assets? There are no assets."

My stomach fell to the ground. The bottom line was this: his business was on life support and we were completely broke. Actually, we were worse than broke. We were broke and in deep debt. He had emptied every one of our personal accounts. Checking, savings, retirement, investments—all dry as a bone. Every penny both of us had worked, scrimped and sacrificed for over the past twenty-two years was unbelievably and irretrievably gone.

"How could you do this?" I wailed, incredulous. "How could you be so completely irresponsible?"

"Oh, typical, blame me," he replied, in his best put-upon, victim voice.

Seriously? Okay, let's review for a moment. Who quit his job without even telling me to start a business he knew nothing about, at the very same time, I might add, that our daughter started college at a pricy private school and that we had just built a new house? Who took out a loan for $2.5 million without telling me? Who borrowed money from private sources to the tune of $900,000, again without telling me? (For the record, I only know numbers that high in terms of fat grams ingested, not dollars owed.) Who lied and deceived me and his investors about the business for more than a year? Who secretly emptied all of our personal accounts, took out a second mortgage on our house, opened and exhausted a new personal line of credit, ran up my credit cards to the tune of $40,000 and lost every single penny of it? And who seemed to have timed it so that he would be out the door before it all came crashing down? Who?

That's what I wanted to say, but all I actually said—through clenched teeth—was, "Well, this *was* all your doing."

"See, this is why I don't like talking to you," he continued while I tried to talk myself out of having a stroke. "You act like it's my fault. I don't have to listen to this negative talk." Then he hung up on me. He was right, I thought, I *was* being negative. I should have said instead, "You are *positively* an irresponsible ass!"

This mind-bending conversation was emblematic of those that would follow in the next weeks and months. In what became a maddening Jekyll and Hyde routine, he would alternately call me to apologize or berate me, depending on which personality inhabited his body at the time. Sometimes he would say how much he missed me, and other times he would say he was glad he was "rid of" me. Sometimes he actually addressed me as "honey" and other times in terms much less affectionate. Once, incredibly, he even called me looking for sympathy because he was lonely. I had emotional whiplash trying to keep up with his moods. And I had no time at all to process the confusion and pain of reconciling this person (or persons) with the man who had talked me through labor, breast biopsies and Torrie's first date. I had spent 20+ years telling myself that what appeared to some—and in my darker moments what I feared—to be deep fissures in Dick's psyche were really only surface cracks that could be filled in with enough love and support. I had wanted so desperately to believe that love could indeed conquer all, and at times, it really *looked* as if it had. But that's what facades are designed to do—*look* good. Regrettably, there is nothing much of substance behind the look. Dick's convincing facade of "normalcy" was splintering before my eyes, starkly revealing how foolish I'd been to believe in a fairy tale.

Unfortunately, and not surprisingly to anyone but me, the unwanted revelations were not limited to financial infidelities. After the first month of separation, Dick and I had reached a precarious equilibrium, resigned to being bound together on paper for a while because of our intertwined finances. There were a number of ways our fate could play out—a new investor and an interested buyer for his business were both hovering in the wings at this time, as well as promising job prospects on the horizon for each of us. We had little choice but to bide our time to see what would pan out. (Editor's note: in the end, nothing did!) Meanwhile, we had at least agreed on a truly austere shared budget to get us through the next few months. So, when he told me he was flying to Minnesota for the weekend to go ice fishing, I was more than a little shocked. Aside from this not being part of our budget, going ice fishing in Minnesota struck me as alien a concept as hiking in Arizona. As usual, he had a quick answer for me. A former colleague was celebrating his 50th birthday and had invited a group of guys up for the weekend, he said. Although Dick had had no contact with this fellow for several years, it was not completely implausible, as they had been very friendly at one time. Still, I was naturally concerned about the cost. He assured me that it was not costing him a penny. The long lost buddy, he explained, once informed of our situation, had insisted on covering the ticket as repayment for all the business Dick had thrown his way in the past. Hmm, Dick was certainly benefitting from the generosity of others. After all, when I had questioned the wisdom of maintaining two households when we were on the verge bankruptcy, he led me to believe that his brother was paying the rent on the apartment, again as repayment for Dick's help in the past. So, off he went to Minnesota.

The next week, Dick called and asked me if I could put together some clothes for him and meet him halfway between my house and his apartment to make the drop. I asked him what clothes he meant since he had made a clean sweep of his closet and drawers on his "high-five" moving day. I winced a little just thinking about that day. He told me he needed some "warm weather" clothes that had been packed away for the season in a spare closet. Hmm, February in Atlanta was considerably milder than February in, say, Minnesota, but not exactly shorts-and-t-shirt weather. He didn't volunteer his destination, but since he and his brother went to Daytona every year about this time for the races, I assumed that was the warm weather spot. I agreed and put together some shorts and shirts for him. Reviewing my selections at our designated meeting spot, the Chick-Fil-A parking lot, he gave each one a thumbs-down. He said he needed nicer things than I had picked out for him. Really? To sit in the bleachers for 24 hours straight at Daytona? I had seen some of the photos from years past and all of guys looked pretty rough by the end of the race weekend. He ended up going to our house the next day while I was at work and getting what he wanted.

One of the very few things I had asked of Dick during this initial separation was that he at least listen to and, if necessary, return messages from me, especially when he was out of town—not for my benefit so much, but we *did*, I seemed to have to remind him frequently, have a daughter who was living away from home, off-campus, in an apartment, driving to and from classes and work, going to parties and engaged in every other activity that puts young people at risk. It was not inconceivable that—heaven forbid—I would need to reach him on her behalf in an emergency. He agreed and told me he would be back from his presumed trip to Daytona on Sunday evening. On Saturday afternoon, Torrie called with a car emergency, one that could be solved with a two-minute conversation with her father, or could end in a $400 mistake. She was at the mechanic, frantic about not being able to reach her father and not knowing what to do. I tried to calm her down, think of a solution and call Dick's cell phone, all pretty much to no avail. Repeated hits of "redial" were fruitless. I figured something had to be wrong with his phone because, while I could easily believe his ignoring my call, it seemed less likely that he would also ignore multiple calls from Torrie. We finally decided to leave her car at the mechanic over the weekend until we consulted her father and she made hasty arrangements for other transportation to work and home.

Meanwhile, I continued to call his cell phone sporadically throughout the rest of the weekend, never getting an answer. There was little I could do but wait for him to return, as he had advised me he would, on Sunday evening. Once home, I was certain he would either 1) answer his phone or 2) call me. Over the course of the weekend, my emotions had run the gamut from annoyed to puzzled to concerned. When I woke for work on Monday morning, with no call from Dick and nothing but the voice mail greeting on his phone, I was really scared that something had happened to him. I checked my phone for messages and tried to call him during every teaching break from 9 a.m. until 9 p.m. Nothing, nothing and more nothing. I was starting to panic, fearing that a terrible fate had befallen him. Surely, I tried to reassure myself, someone would have notified me if something serious had happened. I went home when my class ended at 9 p.m. and alternately tried calling him and sitting with the phone in my lap willing it to ring. I was in bed at about 11 p.m. when I called him one more time and to my great, and short-lived, relief, he answered.

"Oh, thank goodness," I gushed. "Are you okay? We were so worried about you."

He replied that he had missed his plane on Sunday and had had to wait until Monday to get a flight home. Two missed planes in two months, so odd. After again expressing my sincere relief that he was okay, I asked why he had answered neither my calls nor Torrie's.

"My phone wasn't working there," he replied curtly.

"Wasn't working, what do you mean?" I asked.

"I couldn't get a signal on the mountain," he said flatly.

That answer made absolutely no sense.

"Mountain?" I asked, genuinely confused. "Since when is there a mountain in Daytona?"

He paused. "Who says I was in Daytona?" he asked, with an edge in his voice that brought me up short.

"Oh," I said, the catch in my throat as unexpected as his response had been.

There was an uneasy and too-long silence, as I waited for him to volunteer more information. A sharp pang in my stomach, a fluttering of my heart, an unconscious knowing in my soul. And as if in defiance of that knowing, a mental recording looped in my head: "there is no one else, *he promised*; there is no one else, *he promised*; there is no one else, *he promised*." I felt I was teetering at the very brink of a long pier, toes curled tightly around its splintered edge, my final tenuous hold on safety. I had to choose. Turn back and run to solid ground by not asking any more questions or let go and leap into the murky unknown of the sea by asking. In a split second, an impulse more than a decision really, I jumped in.

"Oh, well, where…were…you?" I asked, my voice quivering from the cold and terror of the sea, but hoping for a quick rescue.

His heavy exhale told me I would flounder alone in the darkness; there would be no rope tossed to me.

Strong resistance on his part, desperate insistence on my part and finally the truth—or what passed for truth—emerged. He had been on a mountaintop in *Arizona*—hmm, that sounded familiar—with an old high school girlfriend, with whom he'd been secretly communicating since…since when, he refused to say. Since the time I had needed him to show some concern about my dying father, perhaps? Or maybe since the time I had needed him to help me with my comatose mother? Or was it only since the time I had needed him with me for my "suspicious" mammogram diagnosis? Well, let's just say since the time I had needed him, period, and let it go at that. I was surely the stupidest woman alive.

The betrayal was devastating and brimming with more irony than an O. Henry story. This woman, I'll call her "Honeypot," had surfaced a few times throughout the course of our marriage. (My knowledge of her then consisted mainly of the fact that his parents had not quite approved of her back in the day, deeming her more than a little rough around the edges. Parental disapproval, of course, had only added to the attraction for a rebellious teenage boy—and a screwed up middle aged man, too, I am certain.) She had tracked him down and called his office a time or two in the early years, and once even called me at home, thinking it was his work number. She didn't identify herself to me, but I instinctively knew who it was—mainly by her inelegant speech and obvious ignorance of proper telephone etiquette. ("Hey, who's this, where's Dick at?") From what I could infer from this limited contact, I thought his parents' assessment was generous, ha, ha, but I certainly had one or two questionable skeletons in my own dating closet, so I just laughed it off. Until the call that had come about seven years earlier. That time she called Dick with a wretched tale of woe, which he related to me. Trapped for years in an abusive marriage, she said, she had finally managed to flee her monster of a husband with her *four* children in tow, and was struggling to eke out an existence on the margins of life. Having had no formal education past high school and possessing few marketable job skills, she had taken to "dancing" at a strip club to feed her kids and keep some kind of roof over their heads. Her parents had disowned her, she said, and no one else in her family would help her either. I was completely distraught when I learned of her circumstances. I couldn't even imagine being in such dire straits—how terrifying. And with no one to turn to but an old boyfriend from high school—how humiliating. I accepted her story without question because to my way of thinking the only time a woman would ever swallow her pride and admit this kind of desperation to a former boyfriend was if her children's lives really were at stake. Otherwise, even if she had been reduced to subsisting on a diet of dirt and worms, should she happen to run into an old flame on a subway somewhere, she would lie through her teeth to make her life after him sound fabulous. (My friend and I had actually practiced saying, "Yes, I've just been elected president of the world, as a direct result of your dumping me" with a straight face, in case the need ever arose for either of us.)

In all seriousness, I was concerned for her welfare, but much more so for the welfare of her children. I couldn't bear to think about the seamy characters she surely came in contact with on a daily basis, as her workplace was more Route 12 Truck Stop than *Folies Bergère*.

"What if her kids find out what Mommy does? Do you really think it stops at 'dancing'? What if she is attacked, beaten or murdered by one of her sleazeball customers?" I raged. "She's a Lifetime movie waiting to happen. And her family won't help her? What is wrong with those people?" I demanded to know.

I insisted we help her out somehow, if only for the sake of her children. I couldn't live with myself, I told Dick, if I allowed some latent strain of feminine jealousy to stand between those children and a decent life. As she was living in a city where Dick's company was quite influential, I suggested using his contacts to get her some kind of normal job, doing *something*, *anything*—working in a mailroom had to be better than "dancing." I said I would not be involved in the specifics so as not to embarrass her, but told Dick to do what he thought best—give her some money, be a reference for her or make some calls on her behalf. Unfortunately, I neglected to specifically state that sleeping with her and playing house with her brood while leaving his own family high and dry was not an option. So, yes, the twist of fate seven years later was quite ironic. Never in my wildest dreams had I ever imagined this woman, of all people, to be any kind of threat to my marriage. I mean, Dick traveled constantly in his work and I'm sure encountered all kinds of interesting and attractive women—heck, women I might even leave me for, too—and he was ditching me for *Honeypot*? *Seriously*? After all, not to be unkind, but let's be honest about it—when women worry about "being left," they assume it will be for someone prettier or nicer or smarter than they. We all fear being one-upped, but—allow me this bit of bitchiness— who lives in fear of being one-downed?

But I was not feeling anything close to one-downed flippancy that February night. Whereas Dick's announcement in December that he was leaving had rendered me mute and paralyzed, this revelation had quite the opposite effect. Every nerve in my body felt electrified. Manic energy surged through me. I wanted to run, scream, pound the walls and find some way to release the mounting hysteria. I needed desperately to tell someone what had happened, to rant and rave to someone, but I was alone in my house, and at a little past midnight, I could hardly pick up the phone and expect to find a sympathetic ear, even among my closest friends.

I never closed my eyes that whole night. I frantically paced through the rooms in my house, nervously switching every TV on and off. Back in my bedroom, I flip-flopped on my bed a million times and cried in anguish to Jif. Finally, mercifully, it was morning and time to get ready for work. I had no idea how I was going to function through a full day of teaching, but at least it gave me an agenda, a focus. I had not made a school-wide announcement about the recent developments in my life, but a few of the teachers who were good friends knew the score. They were as shocked as I, to tell the truth, as I had left for Christmas vacation a married woman and had returned a short two weeks later a separated one. It was all so bizarre.

At any rate, I had been holding everything together at work…until that morning. I certainly hadn't planned on falling apart, but I when I walked into the office and someone commented, with genuine concern, that I didn't look so well, my resolve broke. My lip began quivering uncontrollably, and the words came out in gasps. I blubbered the "other woman" news to them, and they all clucked over me appropriately. There are definite benefits to an all-female workplace. And to their extreme credit, not a one said, "I knew it!" though surely all of them had to be thinking it. I pulled myself together and went off to teach my first class. My whole breakdown had taken just under five minutes.

Walking down the hall during class break, I ran into Jose, a former student who had progressed to a higher level English class. I was very fond of Jose and had helped him with paperwork to get his certification as a personal trainer. He was also my back-up plan for my sister if things with Jorge didn't get off the ground. We greeted each other enthusiastically and exchanged hugs. Jose had met Dick some time before at a class party at my house and the two of them had really hit it off. Dick had been the host with the most that night, talking, laughing and playing the happily married man for all he was worth. My students thought he was wonderful. So did I then.

"Oh, I almost forgot, how is your husband doing?" Jose asked, as he was about to return to his classroom. I hesitated and then gave him the *Reader's Digest* version of what had happened. He looked at me, stunned, his mouth agape. I will never forget what he said to me.

"You mean this man left you?" he asked incredulously.

"Yes, he did, Jose," I answered matter-of-factly, nodding my head.

Jose was silent for a moment. Then he looked me in the eye, put his hand on my forearm and said earnestly, "Well, this is a *stupid* man!"

No matter what else Jose may do in his life—become an axe murderer or even marry one of the Real Housewives of Atlanta—he will always be a hero in my eyes.

Thus was the mysterious allure of Arizona explained, and in its immediate wake came several other, smaller, but nonetheless eye-opening, revelations. For example, I learned that not only was Honeypot's ex-husband not abusive, he had paid all the child support and alimony required and was even continuing to cover the medication costs for one of their adult sons—not such a "monster" after all; not only had Honeypot not been "forced" into stripping at the truck stop for a living, she had chosen to do it and was darn proud of it—and she told me she had seen pictures of me and guffawed that I could never have been a stripper...and I had to agree with her on that point; not only had her family of origin not ex-communicated her, she and Dick had attended a family function together in *Minnesota* (former colleague's 50th birthday, my foot!); she and Dick conducted their phone sex, I mean, phone calls, using his office number so there would be no evidence on his cell phone bill and said calls were often exchanged in the morning before many other employees arrived, hence his insistence on going to work on the morning of my mammogram; and, last, but not least, she had, in recent years, acquired a second ex-husband and another child—for whom she was also receiving the agreed-upon child support—and obviously had her sights set on collecting husband number three, namely, mine.

It was, um, a lot of information to digest and the news flashes—and uncovered lies—didn't stop there. The lunacy seemed to update almost hourly. One time Honeypot grabbed Dick's cell phone out of his hand when he was talking to me and threatened, in a voice that obviously well predated, yet nonetheless uncannily mimicked, Honey Boo Boo's, "If you ever call *your* husband on *his* phone when he's at *my* house again, I'll call your school and tell them to fire you!" Huh? Then she twanged out a final warning, "You better cross your 'faaangers', girl."

As mind-boggling and hurtful as the entire situation was, there was one element that was especially troubling to me—Dick's attitude toward Torrie. He had not seen her in person since he had left for his hiking expedition in December, despite my absolutely pleading with him to do so. The first two weekends after his high-five moving day, I asked him to go see her. On both occasions, he said he couldn't afford to "waste" ninety minutes driving over to her college just to talk to her. The third weekend, she was planning on coming home, which would have reduced his drive time to only thirty minutes. I called to tell him and even volunteered to leave the house all afternoon if he wanted to stay there with her instead of trying to have a highly emotional conversation in the middle of Zaxby's. His response to that suggestion was, "Look, I told you, I just don't have time." (Yes, much more efficient use of your time to fly back and forth from Atlanta to Arizona for the weekend rather than drive 28 miles to see your daughter.)

Torrie was profoundly confused, hurt and angry—uh, yeah, I knew that trifecta of feelings pretty well myself. Yet, I knew I had to put aside my own feelings and focus on what was best for her. In those early days, I still had hope that the fever of midlife insanity that had taken hold of Dick would eventually subside and he would return to some sort of normal state. No matter where he and I ended up when all the dust settled, he would still be her father and it was my firm conviction that girls needed their fathers. (Lying, cheating cowards, not so much.) She was ready to slam the door on him forever right then, but I didn't want her to make any rash decisions—out of very justifiable hurt—that might preclude a relationship with him in what I hoped would be the saner future. And so, despite my own feelings, I was put in the peculiar position of, if not defending her father and his indefensible actions, at least petitioning for patience on his behalf.

He made my task increasingly difficult. In addition to flat out ignoring her, he had taken to espousing a host of idiotic new beliefs about "parenting," courtesy of the hardscrabble Honeypot. She was one tough-talking, Jack Daniels-swilling, ass-kicking mama who had no tolerance for, as I once heard her declare in the background of a phone conversation, "crybaby children who didn't carry their weight." I think her motto was something like, "If they're old enough to crawl, they're old enough to trap their own damn dinner!" Adopting her approach to parenting conveniently let Dick off the hook for any responsibility—or guilt—regarding Torrie. Whenever I tried to talk to him about the emotional turmoil she was experiencing, watching all of the values we had fairly pummeled into her all her life—little things like integrity, honor, accountability—being flung into the stratosphere by her father, he would snort some dismissive response.

"Hey, she's a grown-up. Tell her to deal with it. If she doesn't like what I'm doing, that's her problem."

If I told him about repairs she needed on her car, expenses we had normally helped her with, I got, "Hey, the free ride is over. She needs to man up. Life's tough."

Such answers were beyond stupid and absurd on their faces, and much more so coming from him, who, even as he spoke these words, was into his parents, my parents, his siblings and family friends for hundreds of thousands of dollars which he'd "borrowed" to dump into his even more stupid and absurd business. And while his parents' contribution was certainly the largest bailout they had ever provided him, it was far from being the only one they had supplied him over the years. (Not to mention, he had left his partner on the hook for every penny of their shared and staggering business debt.) Yet, somehow he suddenly considered it mollycoddling to help our 20-year-old daughter put working brakes on her car.

Certainly, no one in our families traversed the globe by yacht or private jet, but we hadn't exactly been raised on the mean streets, running from "the man." Neither had our daughter; she'd had the requisite number of Chuck E. Cheese birthday parties, summer camp adventures and dance lessons typical of middle class upbringings. She had been tucked in, snuggled with and had her self-esteem affirmed on a daily basis since birth. Now here was her father, *the same man who once hired a guy dressed in a bear costume to deliver a singing Valentine to her at school,* spewing some kind of ludicrous "kick 'em to the curb" parenting philosophy. His gritty tough guy act was ridiculously incongruous with who he was. I wanted to scream, "Who are you kidding? You are a dentist's son from a small town in Pennsylvania, and until the recent loss of your mind, you were a successful executive who went to church board meetings! For crying out loud, you have no street cred, dude!" It would have been altogether laughable if it hadn't carried such hurtful consequences.

Not to mention, it was not as if Torrie was some kind of delinquent in need of a *Scared Straight* reality check. She was a dean's list college junior, with a part-time job and great friends. She was a hard-working, responsible "good kid," with a bright future. But facts and reason no longer held sway over Dick. He was hiding out in a parallel universe—possibly the one where Jerry Springer guests are spawned. Actually, it was an unheated cabin in a rundown Arizona community of drifters, grifters and assorted other sketchy characters. In his ethically-challenged new world the only limit to how low you would stoop or what line you would cross was how much you could get away with. (Could this really be the same man I had picked wild poppies with on a Tuscan hillside?) Hearing him spout his twisted notions of tough love time and again confirmed to me that he had completed his latest identity transformation. Ever the skilled chameleon, he had done once again as he had most of his life: lacking a strong identity of his own, he had habitually affected the pose of whoever he was with. In his youth, this had meant anyone from boy scouts and athletes to cokeheads and drop-outs. With me, he'd had an extended run, effectively playing the part of the solid citizen and dedicated family man. With the outward trappings of that identity going up in smoke, taking his artificial self-esteem with it and leaving only shame in its stead, he sought refuge in a place where the bar was set pretty close to the ground, where, even at such a low point in his life, he could still feel a bit superior to most everyone around him. A one-eyed man is a king in the land of the blind. And to accompany him in his latest incarnation, he chose as his partner someone who, in his very words to me, "definitely knew she was pretty lucky" to snag him. Apparently, a bankrupt, adulterous, absentee father is considered a good catch for a coarse, adulterous, serial bride. Poor Honeypot thought she had reeled in a big one, believing that Dick had money he had stashed away until after our divorce. That joke was on her, but there very few laughs in it for me either. I guess he fooled us both in different ways.

As if having her rapidly devolving father toss her aside to play daddy to a collection of children whom he'd never even laid eyes on until a couple months earlier wasn't enough of an emotional strain on Torrie, she received yet another crushing blow during this time.

Her boyfriend of a year, with nary a single hint that anything was wrong, just broke up with her, *on the phone*. (What was it with these guerilla-style break-ups? Come out from behind the bushes and dump us like real men!) She was devastated, or re-devastated is more like it, and called me, crying her eyes out. I was out of state at the time, visiting my sisters and mother, and felt so helpless to do much to support her except listen. Of course, it breaks your heart more than they can know to hear your kids suffer, but under normal circumstances, I wouldn't have been overly concerned about her rebounding from a broken romance at 20—I believe one or two people in history have lived through it. But coming at the time that it did, in the way that it did, magnified its impact and brought all the existential questions to bear in a serious way for her.

"They all lie and cheat, mom," she scream-sobbed through the phone. "I will never trust any man ever again in my life. I hate them! I hate them all! I hope they all burn in hell!"

Stock responses of "Now, you know that's not true" and "There are a lot of trustworthy men" rang pretty hollow right then, with the experiential evidence greatly overshadowing the academic at the moment. That was the best I could come up with, though, and she cut me off at the knees.

"Oh, right, mom, like who, Dad? Yeah, like how he said he'd always be there for me, that I could always count on him for anything. That's a joke," she cried.

"I know it's hard to believe right now, but I'm sure your dad loves you. He's just, just very confused right now—"

She cut me off before I could make further feeble attempts at reassurance.

"Mom, stop it! Stop making excuses for him!" she screamed angrily. "You always make excuses for him. You threw your whole life away on him and he takes off with some freaking whore. Stop being stupid!"

Her reaction was a tangle of truth, hurt, exaggeration and defiance, and I knew this was certainly not the time to try to extricate any of those strands, much less to present them to her for evaluation. I was on the phone with her for about an hour, reassuring her that she was more than extraordinary—extra-extraordinary—and that she and I were both strong enough to survive anything any stupid man could throw at us, including a cheap floozy. By the time we hung up, she had calmed down, but the emotional damage was hardly contained. The next weeks, months and years would be incredibly rocky ones for her emotionally. She would unwittingly join the ranks of the walking wounded, attaining all the outward signs of achievement—great job, money, travel—even as she denied the profound hurt inside that was hardening into cynicism.

It was that heart-hardening process that I wanted desperately to prevent. Having failed to protect her from one of life's most painful experiences, I wanted to mitigate the damage in any way possible. I wanted to keep her from using her pain as a whetstone for honing her already sharp wit into a weapon of mass destruction to use against others, ultimately hurting herself the most, of course.

This was my motivation for conjuring up the most preposterously misguided plan for Torrie's 21st birthday celebration. It had been about a month-and-half since the Arizona revelation and a little over three months since her father had announced his exit, and he had yet to spend any significant time with her or have any meaningful communication. As the date drew nearer, I grieved that this milestone birthday, an event that should have been a cause for great joy, would now serve only to emphasize that we were a family divided. When

I thought about Torrie having to ration her time between her father and me on her birthday, it made me very sad for all of us. Instead of a true celebration, her 21st birthday would now serve as the template for all the "split" holidays we would have to look forward to in the coming years. That scenario was weighing heavily on my mind when I opened the newspaper and read that a national touring company would be performing a revival of "Jesus Christ Superstar" on Torrie's birthday. She had wanted to see this show since she had been a little girl taking her first voice lesson. She had had the CD set for years and knew every word of every song. Right then and there I got what seemed like a brainstorm at the time, but, in retrospect, I know was really a complete brain failure. Dick had acted decently to me on a few recent occasions, taking me to get my car fixed, telling me I looked beautiful and even asking if I thought I could "wait for him," i.e., wait until he sorted out the mess he had made and got his life back on track. Maybe, I thought, as a special present for Torrie's birthday, the two of us could take her out for dinner together and then to see the show. He was quite receptive when I approached him with the idea, agreeing that it would be nice not to play tug-of-war over her on her birthday—even though, in reality, he had barely tugged at her at all in the four months since he'd abdicated the throne. Maybe he really was starting to come to his senses, I thought. Maybe the three of us spending an evening together was exactly what we all needed. And so it was with the best of intentions that I put the plan for Torrie's 21st birthday into motion.

The first blow to my good intentions was delivered with Dick's arrival at the door to pick us up. Whatever sentiment had prompted him to treat me decently in recent days—perhaps he and Honeypot had had an argument over where to place "pole" in the bedroom—was long gone by this night. Notorious for mood swings, he'd swung way far from the mood that had possessed him when he told me a few days earlier how much he missed my humor and my kindness in his life.

Things were obviously back on track in the interstate romance department, as he exuded an obnoxious cockiness rarely seen out-side of professional sports and delighted in making oblique refer-ences to his other life, to a "we" that did not include Torrie and me. I had not been prepared for this turning of the tide and, admittedly, I did not handle his repeated jabs well at all. I was obviously not modern or sophisticated enough to sit at dinner with my husband and listen to him talk about his life with his mistress without hav-ing an adverse reaction. The evening became progressively more awkward and uncomfortable, and no amount of Hosanna choruses could reverse the situation. By the time the three of us returned to the house we used to share, my nerves were very much on edge and my sarcasm very much on target. I knew I had to walk away because my uncontrolled barbs were just pouring gasoline on the fire. I went into the kitchen to try to cool off. I was rinsing out a glass at the sink when I heard absolute screams coming out of Torrie's bedroom. I ran back to find her crying hysterically and screaming, "I can't be-lieve you!" while Dick just stood in the doorway, arms at his side, his face expressionless.

I was witnessing my daughter's reaction to her father telling her that he was going to move to Arizona to be with his new "family."

"You can't do that," she screamed. "I need you here! *I* am your family, not your cheap whore. You are *my* father, not theirs!"

I could have killed him on the spot and never felt an ounce of re-gret. Pushing my maternal buttons? Uh, no, more like *smashing* them to smithereens. How dare he say this, do this to her. Not to mention that his plan was completely, completely, well, whatever is stronger than insane, that's what his plan completely was.

Torrie calmed down a bit and told him she didn't care anymore if he wanted to divorce me (hey, throw me under the bus), but that she was still his daughter and she needed him to stay here in Atlanta for now and get her through this critical adjustment. Later, she said, when she was back on solid ground, he could do whatever he wanted.

"I need you here. You can't leave me now," she croaked between sobs.

He just stood there, completely mute, as he routinely did whenever he heard something he didn't want to acknowledge. His eyes narrowed as they always did whenever he decided that no one was going to change his mind or tell him what to do, no matter how ill-conceived his plan. I'd seen that look more times that I could count in the past 23 years.

"Do you hear her? Do you hear what she's saying?" I asked, trying to prod him to respond to her. "She's not asking for your whole life, just for some time with you now. Then you can go live however you want, with whomever you want. Surely, your daughter is worth that."

His continued standing there mute. Finally, he announced that there was nothing here for him anymore, that his life was elsewhere.

That sent Torrie over the edge again (and me as well, but I tried to hold my tongue). "What do you mean there's nothing here for you? I am here!" she screamed.

"Well, I can't be here and there at the same time," he said finally.

"Then you have to make a choice. Who's more important to you, me or Arizona?" she cried, putting air quotation marks around the word "Arizona."

The silence of his reply was deafening. Without saying a word, he simply turned around and headed down the hall to the front door. Hearing Torrie's tortured cry swelling over his departing footsteps hurt worse than having the flesh torn from my bones.

I admit that I completely lost it then and ran after him, telling him he could not just walk out like a coward again. He continued out the door, saying nothing, not turning around, not acknowledging me at all. I followed him down the sidewalk to his car, parked on the street.

"You selfish bastard," I yelled as he opened the car door to get in. He was just going to drive off without another thought. "How can you do this to her? Do you really want her to think it's acceptable to treat her like this? Is this the pattern you want to create for her relationships with men?" I madly grabbed at his shirt to keep him from leaving, to make him face up to the damage he was inflicting.

"You don't tell me what to do," he barked, arching his body away from me and successfully eluding my grasp. I wobbled a bit and then dropped my arms at my side, defeated.

"You have totally lost your mind!" I screeched, stomping the ground and flinging my arms in frustration.

In an instant, he swung his forearm arm at me forcefully, smacking me directly across the chest and knocking me off balance to the ground. A bit of Jerry Springer drama right there in our fancy gated community. Shame on both of us.

And that is how my leg came to be bruised, how my black skirt came to be torn and how I came to be looking up from the asphalt at the complete stranger who used to be my husband on the night of my daughter's 21st birthday. And that is also how I came to know, deep in my soul, that no matter how many more moods my estranged husband would swing through, or how many more U-turns into and out of decency he would make, there would be only one direction for me—straight ahead, with no going back.

5

Dedicated to the One I Love

WHEN I WALKED in to teach my English as a Second Language class that Tuesday night in October 2001, I had no idea how it would change my life. If someone had told me at the end of that first class that one of the people in the room would have a significant impact on my life, I would have felt a surge of excitement, believing my matchmaking efforts on my sister's behalf would prove successful. I had mentally picked out Jorge, the handsome Colombian man in the first row, for her within the first 30 minutes of class, as soon as I'd found out he was divorced—and had no small children. I hatched a scheme right then to get the two of them together and let nature take its course. He had no clue, or say in the matter, but I had pretty much mapped out the rest of his life.

For her part, my sister was willing to take Jorge sight unseen because, well, partly because she was having zero luck finding anyone suitable on her own, but mainly because he was Grade A Prime material. Smart, sexy, well-mannered, sexy, with a good sense of humor. Plus, he was very sexy. And over and above all of these qualifications, he possessed the one thing that made both of us swoon, the thing that would have made her follow him off the edge of a cliff—an accent. I often tell my male ESL students not to lose every trace of their accents because I believe it gives them a real edge with American women. Most American women I know are absolute suckers for a man with a foreign accent. Honestly, I am such an accent junkie I still get a little weak in the knees over Pepe LePew.

Alas, somewhere between point A and point B, my plan went off track. No matter how carefully I tried to orchestrate meetings between my sister and Jorge, something always went awry at the last minute, and several months into my master plan, the two had yet to meet. I tried to maintain a friendship with Jorge to keep the door open for my sister, but eventually his work schedule changed and he no longer attended English classes where I taught. Meanwhile, concerned about the increasing distance Dick seemed to be putting between us, I had decided that I should not teach night classes any more, that it was more important for me to be home with him. I told my boss I needed to switch my schedule to all day classes. I had no idea at the time that I would soon be sitting home at night all by myself. It was just Jif and I every night, sitting and staring into 4,000 square feet of emptiness during the early weeks of 2003.

One night in late January, my boss called me and said she knew I didn't want to be away from home at night, but she wanted to know if I would do her a giant favor by taking over one night class. It seemed the instructor hired to teach the class had walked out—just walked out, with no warning—after the first night. (There was a lot of that going around!) The poor class had had a different substitute every night since, and they were hopelessly behind and discouraged.

"Actually," I told my boss, "my situation has changed and I would be delighted to take over the class. And you can put me back on the night schedule permanently."

It was a true godsend to have somewhere to be at night. I inherited a wonderful class and enjoyed working with them tremendously. At break time that first night, I went to the school's food court and saw several of my former students and chatted happily with them. The time that I spend teaching adult ESL classes is like time out of mind for me. I get to take a trip around the world without ever leaving town and the students are so appreciative and anxious to learn—a teacher's dream. It is impossible not to have your spirits buoyed by the whole experience. So I was walking a little lighter on my feet as I left the food court at the end of the break when I heard someone call my name. I turned around and Jorge was standing behind me. We were surprised to see each other because neither of us was scheduled to be there. He explained that he had a new job that enabled him to attend evening classes again. I briefly explained why I was there, and then we had to hurry back to our classes so we wouldn't be late.

Over the next few weeks, Jorge and I would talk during breaks, and I filled him in on the details of what was going on with my marriage. He was nearly as shocked as I about how suddenly, strangely and one-sidedly everything had taken place. He listened sympathetically and counseled me strongly to do whatever I could to save my marriage. He was speaking from experience, he said, when he told me that even when divorce is the "best" decision, it is terribly difficult. He said it was impossible to overestimate the heartache involved, especially to your kids, even when they were very nearly adults. No matter how many people you know who have gone through it or how prepared you think you are, he said, you can't imagine how it rips your life apart. He was so kind and so wise, it was a shame he was probably not going be my brother-in-law. My sister had developed some serious health complications that put dating plans on the back burner.

I saw Jorge at break time a couple of days after I had found out the truth about Arizona.

"Men are such lying, cheating jerks," I said with disgust.

Jorge strongly nodded in agreement and said very seriously, "Yes, it is for this reason that I prefer the women."

He scored with that line, getting me to laugh with him. I felt so comfortable with him that I told him about the secret plan I'd had to "give" him to my sister.

"Maybe it is my English," he said. "Maybe I don't understand. How you can give me to someone? What if I don't agree?"

"Oh, you get no say in the matter," I said, laughing. "My sister and I had already decided everything for you."

"Oh, good to know," he said, shaking his head. "But I think your plan has a mistake."

"What do you mean?" I asked, genuinely.

"I think you give me to the wrong sister," he replied, smiling.

"Oh, really?" I said lightly and we both laughed. Then break was over.

I didn't give a second thought to what Jorge had said, assuming it was some mild flirting just for fun or maybe to make me feel less rejected. I also knew that as kooky as this sounds, as an ESL teacher, your students can get overly attached to you; a sort of transference, not unlike what therapists encounter, can happen. This is particularly true when someone who is well-educated, with a very successful career and full life, is forced, for political or other reasons beyond his control, to flee his country. He arrives here accustomed to a certain lifestyle and social status and finds he is on the very bottom of the pile, doing some menial job and looked down on by people who don't have half the education he does, simply because he doesn't speak English yet. It is a thoroughly demoralizing experience. And then he comes to an ESL class, where the teacher is very familiar with his type of situation and treats him as the accomplished individual that he is. The teacher becomes his salvation and takes on a disproportionate importance in his life for a period of time. I have both witnessed and experienced this phenomenon several times, so I didn't take Jorge's comments too seriously.

One night a few weeks later, I was walking down the hall with Jorge and another student, showing them where they needed to go for some information. On the way, we walked past Hope, another teacher, who was standing at her classroom door. The three of us were laughing and talking and we waved to her as we hustled down the hall. Later that night when all the teachers were signing out, Hope made a few teasing remarks about my "boyfriend." I didn't know what she was talking about.

"The guy you were walking down the hall with earlier," she said.

I honestly didn't know who she was talking about. I looked at her quizzically.

"The guy you were with when you went past my room at break," she explained.

"Oh," I said, as it clicked with me. "That's not a guy; that's Jorge. He's the one I was going to give to my sister."

"Well, he wasn't thinking about your sister tonight," she said, arching her eyebrow at me.

"Oh, you're crazy," I replied dismissively. "I think he did have an 'ESL crush' awhile ago, but he's just a friend."

"Honey," she continued, "he was checking you out the whole time, and *not* like a friend. Your wacko hubby better get his act together because I know someone who is ready to take his place."

I laughed, "You're nuts!"

"That I am, but I'm not wrong," she said and we both laughed.

One Thursday night a few weeks later, my car happened to be parked near Jorge's in the school lot. When I was getting in my car to go home, he called good night to me.

"Good night," I called back. "I'll see you Tuesday."

He walked over to my car then and said, "Really, I have to wait until Tuesday? What about Friday or Saturday or Sunday?"

At first I thought he was kidding, but the look on his face told a different story. I was a bit taken aback and wasn't sure how to respond. I sort of stumbled around and he rescued me, for the first of many times.

"We can go to a movie or to the park," he suggested.

'Well, okay, sure, yeah, okay. You have my number, call me tomorrow and we can decide what to do," I said.

I got in my car and realized I was shaking! I don't remember driving home that night. I ran in the house and immediately emailed my friend Suzi, panicked about what this meant, what to say, how to act. I didn't know if I should actually go through with it or make up an excuse. I was married—okay, obviously, it was more of a technicality at that point, but I still held out hope that Dick would come back to earth. At the very least, I was not ready to begin a "relationship." All this and pages more, I poured out to her in my email.

My panic and monumental overreaction must have translated well electronically because she called me about two seconds after I sent the email.

"Get a grip, girl," she said when I picked up the phone. "It's literally a walk in the park that he's proposing, not marriage."

"Or the movies, don't forget the movies, and it's dark in the movies!" I countered, with the emotional voice of a 7th-grader.

"You've known him for over a year, and you've had coffee with him before," she said with frustration.

"That was different, and you know darn well it was!" I replied with just as much frustration. "Plus, I had diet Coke, not coffee, so that's how much you know, Miss Smartie Panties!"

She eventually convinced me that accepting Jorge's invitation would not necessarily knock the Earth off its axis. Anything was always possible, of course, but the chances were slim. So, I decided I would go, but stay only in public places. I further decided I would drive my own car and meet him there, wherever we determined there would be. I hoped those moves would keep the Earth from wobbling off course as well as protect my soul from the eternal damnation I deserved for temporarily seeking my own happiness despite having being raised Catholic. Jorge called, and since the weather report predicted rain all weekend, we voted down the park idea and decided to meet at the movies right around the corner from my house on Friday evening. To this day, I, who can remember what color of eye shadow my sister's friend's cousin wore to her high school's Homecoming Dance in 1967 (when I was 10 years old), cannot remember what movie Jorge and I saw that night. I can't remember walking into the theatre, walking out or anything at all that happened in between. I remember only one thing—the kiss. Oh, dear. It was every cliché in the book. Full-on heart-pounding, head-spinning, spine-tingling, weak-in-the-knees wonderment. I had not been kissed by anyone besides Dick since 1979. And I hadn't been kissed by him—more than a perfunctory peck—for quite some time. And I had *never* been kissed by *anyone*, in my whole life *ever*, like that first kiss from Jorge.

Somehow, afterward, I got in my car and very nearly floated home. I remember leaning back in the car seat after I was safely in my garage, closing my eyes and reliving the moment in slow motion about a million times before getting out and going in the house. Good grief, I thought, when I finally opened my eyes again, I am 45 years old and I am swooning. How ridiculous, embarrassing, and, oh, so completely wonderful.

A step at a time, from then on, Jorge moved closer and closer to the center of my life. I often felt guilty that he had jumped on board my sinking ship. He had just had just barely survived having had a bomb dropped on his own life. He had been the vice president of the international division of a bank in Colombia and had detected and reported a money laundering operation, a very courageous, but extremely dangerous, thing to do in Colombia in the late '90s when drug-traffickers and anti-government guerilla forces were at the height of their power. Death threats by phone soon followed and even body guards were not enough to deter the bad guys. As he was driving home alone one evening, three Mercedes sedans appeared seemingly out of nowhere and blocked him in on a side street. Within seconds he was pulled from his car by four guerilla thugs and had three guns pointed at him. After cursing him out for interfering with their operation, they told him to prepare to die, and brought their three pistols to rest against his forehead and temples, their fingers twitching at the triggers. And then, a split second before blowing his brains out, they began violently pistol whipping him instead, shattering his forehead and causing him to collapse on the pavement. They kicked and punched him repeatedly and left him in a bloody heap on the side of the street. In another second they were gone and so was his car— along with his wallet, computer and cell phone. A cab driver found him and rushed him to the hospital where doctors worked to put him back together, but his life was changed irrevocably. He was faced with a painful decision. If he stayed in Colombia, he risked not only his own life, but possibly his two sons' lives as well. He hated leaving them—young adults, but still needing their father—but he had little choice. He was granted temporary political asylum in the U.S., but soon found that any job in finance made him too visible when he got a phone call after working in New York, saying "we know where you are." Ever since that call, he had been living in Atlanta with his brother and keeping a very low profile. It was obvious how much he missed his boys, but other than that, I never heard him express any anger or bitterness about the losses he had sustained. When I said how hard it must have been to let go of all his accomplishments and achievements, and live a considerably downsized life in a place he had never intended to be, he simply answered, "But now I can breathe."

Despite the giant upheaval he'd just endured in his own life, he signed on to help me pick up the pieces of my decimated life as well. He did so even though for the first several months I made it clear that if Dick suddenly returned to his senses, I would do whatever I could to save my marriage.

"We are separated right now, but it's very early in the game," I told him. "We are not divorced and this may not be the end of the story."

He said he understood clearly, but, he added, in the meantime, he couldn't possibly walk away from me because he had been in love with me since the first night that I walked into his classroom. I laughed at what seemed to me a flattering but obvious lie or at least exaggeration.

"Oh, please. You never gave any hint or clue for the whole first year that I knew you," I said.

"Do not forget that I am an expert poker player," he replied with such gravity that I actually believed him.

Jorge positioned himself between me and the disasters befalling me on a seemingly daily basis from the very start. Two incidents in particular in those very early days of our relationship defined his heart and character to me—and made his decency stand out in high relief against Dick's lack thereof. I had hired a small lawn maintenance company to help me rein in the out-of-control growth of my yard. They came and tackled the big jobs I needed to have done while

I was at work. When I returned home from teaching that day, I walked around to inspect the job. It looked better, but there was a very strong smell of natural gas on one side of my house. Following my nose, I determined the smell to be coming from the spot where the lawn guys had dug up a shrub to relocate it. I had to be back at school in a few hours to give the final exam—why did disasters always seem to fall during final exam week?—so I needed to move quickly to address a dangerous situation. I immediately called the gas company, and they dispatched someone to me almost immediately. He determined that the leak was coming from the part of the line that was my responsibility to fix and, although he could not say officially, he agreed it was almost certainly coming from a break near where the lawn guys had dug up my shrub. I asked him who could fix it and he told me to call a plumber. When he left and I went inside, the smell of gas was very noticeable, especially in the dining room, as the leak was right under one of the dining room windows. I was scared I was going to blow up. I called the lawn guy and he refused to do anything, saying only that I couldn't prove that his crew had caused the leak and then he pretty much hung up on me. I didn't have time to argue, as I had to be back at work shortly. I decided I would just turn the gas off since it was summer and I didn't need heat and get the problem taken care of the next day. At least in the meantime I could leave for class and not worry that poor Jif was being gassed or that the house was going to explode in my absence.

There was only one problem—I had no idea where the gas shut-off valve was. I hated myself for being so house-stupid, but I didn't know what the valve looked like, if it was outside the house, inside the garage or if there was any trick to turning it off. I needed to contact Dick and ask him, but he was hiding out atop his Arizona trash heap that week, which meant his cell phone would not have a signal. The only other way to reach him was to call the phone in Honey's cabin/hut. I actually had that number—I had called directory assistance to get it awhile back when Torrie had needed some information—but when I had called him that time, he informed me that he and

Honeypot *forbade*, yes, *forbade*, his exact word—and I say "his" and not "their" since I don't think Honeypot knew the past tense of "forbid"—me from ever calling there again. It didn't matter if I was in the emergency room with our daughter bleeding out, I was not to disturb their idyllic life, *ever*, under threat of prosecution! Prosecution for what, I have no idea, as I had committed no crime other than criminal stupidity. I decided I would call my future ex-sister-in-law, who was a very decent and reasonable person, and ask her if she would call her brother, ask him where the shut-off valve was and call me back. It sounded easy, but it wasn't. My future ex-father-in-law had issued a gag order to the whole family of *adult* children—no one was to speak to me, at all, ever, without his permission. I am not kidding, this is the God's honest truth. First of all, what grown person does that, and second of all, what grown people abide by such a directive? This is the level of insanity I was dealing with. These people had been my supposed family for the past 23 years and now I was *persona non grata*. I certainly understand the whole "blood is thicker" deal, and I was not asking anyone to get in the middle of things or "be on my side," but acting as if Dick's behavior was perfectly acceptable while characterizing me as untouchable—as well as my former mother-in-law telling my own daughter that I "deserved" what Dick had done—was unbelievably hurtful as well as maddening. I wanted to scream, "*I* am not the one who has behaved despicably here!"

Anyway, once I got through the call-screening system—someone else had answered the phone and interrogated me about why I was calling there and what I wanted—and my sister-in-law got on the phone, she agreed to help me out. She said she would call her brother and then call me back. I waited and waited, but no return call came before it was time for me to go to class. There was no way I could be late for class because I actually had the final tests with me. I didn't know what to do and was close to giving in to my desire to just sit down on the floor and cry until the gas fumes put me out of my misery, but there Jif to consider. At that point, I just figured that my sister-in-law had been unable to contact her brother yet, but I still believed that she would eventually call me back and leave a message while I was at class. I could think of no one else to turn to, so I called Jorge and explained the situation to him. I told him I would keep checking my voice mail for messages while my students tested. I asked him if he would mind terribly driving down to my house—about a half-hour drive for him—and turning off the gas valve once I found out where it was located.

He not only said he would, he told me that he knew where my valve was—or knew where it should be—and would go to my house to turn it off right then, no need to wait for a call that might not ever come. He also told me he would repair the leak for me the next day. Had I forgotten, he asked, that he in addition to degrees in economics and marketing, he also had a degree in civil engineering? Fixing a leaky gas line was well within his skills set, he said. I was so relieved that I almost started crying. When I got home from class nearly four hours later, the gas had been turned off, the smell had dissipated and Jif was none the worse for wear. I checked and double-checked my home phone, and there was no message, or even call, from my sister-in-law. I called her to find out what had happened and she said that she had not actually called her brother. She had, instead, called her father—the gag order and all—and asked him what to do. He had directed her not to call me back, but to offer me this sage advice if I called her again. He said, and I quote. "If the leak is inside the house, tell her to open the windows."

Thanks.

Jorge went to my house the next day to fix the leak while I was at school. He was lying on the ground, mending the line, having already laid down a bed of stones, as per code, when a car pulled into the driveway. It was Torrie, making an unscheduled and unannounced visit home from college to pick up a few things. She got out of the car, very confused and concerned about the strange man lying on the ground beside the house. For his part, Jorge was surprised and nervous because I had not told him that Torrie would be coming home. This was not the first impression he had wanted to make. She walked around to the side of the house cautiously. Jorge jumped up and dusted himself off as best he could.

"Hello," said Torrie uncertainly.

When Jorge answered and she heard his accent, she asked, "Are you Jorge?"

"Yes," he answered. "And are you Torrie?"

"Yes," she said.

"It's very nice to meet you," Jorge told her. "I didn't know you were coming today."

"No, I just decided at the last minute," she explained. Then, she asked, "Um, does my mom know that you are here? And, like, digging a hole in our yard?"

Jorge laughed and explained what he was doing. At that, she let out a big sigh of relief, that 1) he wasn't a serial killer digging a makeshift grave and 2) he was taking care of things for me. Their relationship was off and running.

Not too long after the gas leak incident, I spent two weeks back in my hometown in Pennsylvania, closing on the sale of my parents' house. My father had been gone a little over a year by then, and it was clear that my mother, who had moved in with my sister in Florida ten months earlier, was never going to return to live in the house. My two sisters, my mother and I all flew in from our various locations to pack up the house and close the door on the fifty years of history that had passed under that roof. It was an emotionally and physically grueling two weeks, and my dissolving marriage made the experience all the more poignant for me. We closed on the sale at the end of the second week and spent the last two nights of our stay at my cousin's house. We needed to get my mother's car down to Florida, so the plan was for me to drive it to Atlanta and then my nephew would fly up from Florida and drive the car back. I had not slept very much during the two weeks we were there and the last night, between emotional turmoil and my sinuses being sealed shut from all the smokers in the house, I got no sleep at all. I couldn't imagine how I was going to get in the car and drive twelve hours, but that's what I had to do. Those twelve hours expanded into eighteen of the most miserable in my life.

I had planned to leave around 8:00 in the morning, which would have put me back in Atlanta by about 8:00 that evening. I had made this drive many times, so I knew it was twelve hours just about on the nose. After getting zero sleep, I got out of bed around 6:00 that morning to pack up the remaining items in the car. When I started the car to pull closer to the garage, the "check engine" light came on. I couldn't even believe what I was seeing, as I had just had the car serviced. I had to wait until 7:00 to call the dealership. They told me to bring the car in at 10:00. My arrival time was pushed back later and later and I hadn't even left yet. Long story, short—by the time they figured out and fixed the problem, it was 12:30 p.m. Okay, I thought, I won't get home until 12:30 a.m., but I can handle that. I pulled out of the dealership two-and-a-half hours behind schedule and realized that I was hungry. I pulled into the Wendy's drive-thru lane to grab a quick bite. Ten years later, I still remember this scene so clearly. I was miserably tired and cranky from no sleep; my hair, clothes and very skin reeked of cigarette smoke, making me even crankier; my emotional footing was dissolving under me, with my childhood home gone and my present-day home on very shaky ground. Feeling the full brunt of all of these factors as I pulled into the drive-thru lane, I had no patience for even the slightest irritation, which is why I thought I reacted so strongly when the seat belt snapped against my left breast as I stepped on the brake.

"Ouch, crap," I yelped aloud. "That really hurt," I continued, talking to no one except myself.

Stupid period boobs, I thought absentmindedly, as I pulled up to order. I started mentally calculating when my period was due as I yanked a couple of dollars out of my wallet. Suddenly, a pang of fear shot through me as I realized that I had actually just had my period, so my breast should not have been sore at all. Having had so many breast issues before, I immediately became concerned. I pulled into a parking space and felt the top of my breast where the seat belt had snapped me. It was rock hard and very painful. I was panic-stricken.

I immediately ran to the bathroom inside Wendy's to examine what was going on. What I saw knocked my knees out from under me and I collapsed onto the toilet seat. There was an area about the size of a half-dollar, encompassing part of my nipple, which was red, hard, swollen and very painful. It was even hot to the touch. I was terrified. I ran back out to my car and grabbed my cell phone to call my gynecologist and schedule an appointment for the next day. I got the voice mail, informing me calls would not be answered until after lunch at 2:00 p.m. By 2:00 p.m., I had hit a severe thunderstorm in West Virginia, which, combined with the mountainous terrain, made sustaining a cell phone signal all but impossible. It was also not at all wise for me to keep placing repeated calls on my phone while driving on rain-soaked, serpentine roads. The couple of times I hit a break in the storm, I tried to call, but lost the signal while I was on hold. Meanwhile, the pain in my breast was getting worse and worse, and the area was even more swollen, resembling a golf ball cut in half.

I was frustrated and scared. I would have called Jorge and asked him to call the doctor for me, but 1) he was at work and I didn't know that number 2) it was a pretty daunting task for a second-language speaker and 3) it was a little more information than I felt comfortable sharing. I couldn't afford to keep stopping and wasting more time on my already very behind-schedule trip, and I had to get an appointment set up. I called Dick—who, according to what he'd last told me, was in Atlanta, throwing the last shovel of dirt on his dead business, so it was "legal" to call him—on his cell phone and actually got through. I quickly explained the situation and asked him to please call for me. Though not in the least sympathetic, he did agree to do it. I lost the signal on my phone at the end of that call and did not recover it until several hours later, long enough to listen to Dick's message telling me I had a gynecologist appointment at 9:00 the next morning. The storms in West Virginia gave way to a miles-long traffic snarl of accidents in North Carolina, all of which put me in South Carolina in the midst of a deluge at about 11:00 p.m. It was one of the worst downpours I have ever seen. The shoulder of the interstate was clogged with cars that had given up trying to drive through the high water and zero visibility. I tried to push on, but it was becoming dangerous to the point of foolhardiness. I wanted to pull over, but there were no open spaces anywhere. Just ahead, however, there was an exit, so I got off the interstate there and hoped there would be a gas station or fast food place where I could safely wait out the latest wave of rain...and go to the bathroom! I had to have picked the most desolate exit on the entire interstate. I saw nothing that looked remotely safe or welcoming as I followed a truck ahead of me to some lights in the distance. The lights turned out to belong to a cement block complex with a "Food" sign atop the small building in front and a "Girls Girls Girls" sign atop the bigger one in back. I was the only car among a village of 18-wheelers, and, as far as I could tell, the only woman in the crowd—outside of those presumably in the "Girls Girls Girls" building. I am sure there are thousands of very nice, respectable looking truckers, and not one of them was in that parking lot at midnight in the middle of a blinding rainstorm. I was, instead, surrounded on all sides by very seedy-looking characters, several of whom were taking leering note of my presence, which was scaring the daylights out of me. My bladder was close to rupturing, my back and tailbone were throbbing, and the golf ball in my left breast was on fire with pain, but I certainly couldn't get out of the car there. I double-checked my door locks and pulled out of there as fast as I safely could.

It was 1:00 a.m. I was beyond exhausted and still three hours from home—in good weather. I didn't think I could drive one more mile. When I got back on the interstate, there were still some vehicles parked on the side of the road, but the rain had let up some, and a stream of cars was heading to the next exit, apparently attracted by the bright lights of a Holiday Inn Express. (Just my luck, I had gotten off one exit too soon before, trading the safety of a Holiday Inn for Girls, Girls, Girls.) I got off too, deciding to catch a few hours of sleep and get up in time to drive straight to my gynecologist's office in the morning—well, later in the same morning, actually. By the time I got there, the rain had started up again, and I got 100% soaked running across the parking lot. I opened the door of the lobby—dripping wet, smelling like an ash can, with a stiff back, full bladder and a golf ball in my breast—to see about seven people in line ahead of me. I prayed there were at least eight rooms left. The line continued to grow, with a young couple and crying baby directly behind me. When I reached the counter, the desk clerk announced that I had gotten the last available room. I couldn't believe it; for once, I was the winner. I felt like a skunk, though, as the young couple with the crying baby clearly needed a room, too. I debated for a few moments and then behaved completely selfishly and took the room for myself! Amid loud groans and grumbles, the desk clerk directed everyone behind me down the interstate a few exits to another hotel. I felt so bad, I wanted to turn to the crowd and announce, "Please, don't hate me. I have a golf ball growing in my breast!"

After three of the most fitful hours of sleep in the history of the world, I got up and drove the rest of the way home, arriving in the parking lot of my gynecologist's office at 8:45 a.m. I was quite a sight, but, fortunately, everyone in the office had known me for years, so they didn't judge me too harshly. As thoroughly scared as I was by the ball in my breast, I was still, almost unconsciously, looking forward to my gynecologist, if not dismissing, at least minimizing, my fear. For ten years, through every lump, bump, and shadow, she had always been the voice of reason. Even when the radiologist's initial report had been concerning, my gynecologist always said something like, "I really think you're okay, but it's best to be extra cautious."

When the nurse called me back, I ran into my doctor in the hallway on the way to the exam room.

"So, what's going on with you?" she said, cheerfully. "Did you feel another cyst?"

"No, I don't know what this is," I said, as I pulled the scoop neck of my shirt down enough for her to see the top of my breast.

She took a deep breath, took me by the elbow and steered me into the exam room. She lifted up my shirt and studied the "ball" for a moment without saying anything.

"What do you think?" I asked shakily, mentally begging for her to say, "Oh, that's just such-and-such. It looks bad, but isn't serious."

But she didn't. She said, "Okay, you are going to go downstairs and get a mammogram and ultrasound right now and then go straight to the surgeon from there and let him evaluate this. I'm going to go make the calls now."

I couldn't believe what I was hearing. Fear wrenched my stomach. Say the thing, I thought as hard as I could. Say the thing you always say. Please say, "Just being very cautious."

But she said nothing, and I couldn't bear its absence. I spoke and named the fear that had been relentlessly pounding in my head since Wendy's bathroom, making it much more real that I was prepared to handle.

"Do you think this looks like inflammatory breast cancer?" I was trying to give her another chance to dismiss my fears.

"I think we just need to get you downstairs and then over to the surgeon," she non-answered. "You wait here and I'll be right back."

The door clicked shut and I was totally alone in the examination room. Exhausted and frightened out of my wits, I completely broke down, crying, shaking and whispering a prayer over and over, "Please, no, please, no, please, no." I couldn't sit, I couldn't stand and I couldn't stay inside my skin. And I most certainly couldn't do this by myself. But I had no one to call. All of my girlfriends were at work. Jorge was at work too. My sisters were hundreds of miles away. I didn't know what to do. I finally called Dick, just needing to hear a familiar voice. Despite his present insanity, he had always been a strong support during my many breast scares in past years. He answered and I poured out what was going on.

"And she (my doctor) has never acted like this. She must really be worried. I am so, so scared, just so scared. I don't think I can do this alone right now..." and then my voice was consumed by sobs.

He was silent on the other end of the line. And then he inhaled and said, "Well, good luck to you," and hung up.

I stood in the middle of the room, holding my cell phone in my hand, feeling more alone than I had ever felt before. The door opened then and my doctor told me I was scheduled for a mammogram and ultrasound downstairs in 45 minutes and from there I would go, films in hand, to the breast surgeon.

Somehow, I managed a weak joke, asking her to write me an excuse for the way I looked and smelled, so the people in the imaging center wouldn't turn me away. She smiled and told me that they had seen—and smelled—even worse.

I went outside and sat on a bench and did something I had never done before. I called Jorge at work. When he picked up his line, I told him everything that was going on and before I could even ask him if he would come, he asked me if he could. I explained where I was and he said he'd leave work immediately. He would likely not be able to get there before I went in for the mammogram, but he'd be waiting there for me afterward, he said, and would go with me to the surgeon. I was so grateful and relieved that I wouldn't be alone. I went and checked into the imaging center.

When my name was called, I walked back with the technologist and tried not to think about how incredibly painful this mammogram was going to be. No picnic under ordinary circumstances, I shuddered to think what it would feel like smashing this golf ball between two plates today. The procedure did not disappoint; it was excruciatingly painful, times four. Tears ran down my cheeks as I whimpered quietly through each compression. Finished with that torture, I went on to the ultrasound, and then dressed and waited for the films. Films in hand, I walked down the long hallway leading back to the waiting room. I had a flashback of the last time I had made this walk, the day I had found Dick slumped in a chair, sleeping. I opened the door this time and immediately saw Jorge sitting in a chair nearby, with his eyes fixed in my direction. He got up and came to me with his arms open wide. I melted. I had never been so happy to see someone in my whole life. I still knew nothing of my diagnosis, but I was not alone any more. From there, he went with me up a couple of floors to the surgeon. I had seen this breast surgeon more than a few times over the years since I had first start-ing having breast issues in my late 30s. I liked him and, as it turned out, he had always been the bearer of good news. I hoped that today would not be different. I sat on edge of the examination table as he looked over the films. Then he examined me.

"Have you had any kind of breast injury in the past few days?" he asked. "Anything that broke the skin?

"No," I said. "This just came up yesterday, out of nowhere," I answered. And then, I thought a moment. Suddenly, I had a memory, a flash of an image in my mind, of me getting rammed in the breast with the sharp corner of a heavy box while packing up my mother's house the week before. So much had transpired in the past two weeks that it all ran together in my mind. "Well, maybe I did get hit in the breast."

He told me that he suspected I had a very bad infection and he was going to draw out some fluid and go from there.

I felt a little relieved that there could be an alternate explanation besides a deadly disease. I had had many suspected cysts drained before, so I knew that if the needle went in and clear-to-grayish fluid came gushing out, it was usually a good sign. What you didn't want was the needle to go in and nothing, or maybe blood, to come out. That was not a good sign. The surgeon plunged the needle in, and for the first time in many years of needle pokes, nothing, nothing at all, came out.

I gasped, and let out a cry, "Oh, no, that's not good."

I felt like I was going to faint, and, in fact, a second later, just after he withdrew the needle, I did exactly that. The nurse caught me as I was falling back and laid me flat on the examination table. A few moments later, I was okay.

"A very common vagal nerve response," the surgeon explained. "Nothing to worry about there."

As for the lump with no fluid, he continued, it was not an unusual finding when there was a lot of infection present. The consistency tended to be more gelatinous than fluid, he said. Ten years later, I even remember exactly how he worded it.

"Things can get really *squirrely* in there," he said. Squirrely? Obviously a medical term.

He further explained that he was going to start me on a round of antibiotics. Once the infection cleared up, then he could tell if there was anything else going on. He sent me home and told me that if by morning the lump was noticeably reduced, I was to finish the course of antibiotics and then come back. If the lump had not responded to the antibiotics at all by morning, then I needed to call him immediately.

I left there feeling completely wrung out. Jorge put me in my car and sent me home, thankfully a very short distance, while he took the prescription to the drug store and waited to have it filled. Per Jorge's instructions, I took a shower, washed my hair and put on clean— smoke-free!—clothes. He arrived shortly after, gave me the pills, and insisted on taking me to get a decent meal. At dinner, I told Jorge that if my situation turned out to be something very serious, I wanted him to know he was under no obligation to stay with me. We weren't married, engaged or even going steady. Shoot, I was still legally married and he owed me nothing.

He screwed up his face and said almost angrily, "What? You are crazy! I love you and I am not going anywhere. And what's more, you are going to be fine."

Then he took me home, ordered me to bed and instructed me to call him first thing in the morning—and further ordered me not to examine the lump every ten seconds! He knew me well.

Mercifully, exhaustion trumped anxiety, and I not only fell asleep, but also slept through the entire night. I woke up about 7:30 the next morning, petrified to look inside my pajama top. I just lay on my back for several minutes, trying to work up my nerve to proceed. Finally, I held my breath and took a peek. While obviously still there, the lump was appreciably smaller. I went limp with relief. In the end, it took three weeks of antibiotics to clear the infection up completely and to reveal that there was no underlying issue. Jorge brought me roses and took me out to dinner to celebrate—at which point, I called my sister and told her that my initial instincts about Jorge had been right on target; he was a keeper. And—so sad, too bad for her—I was definitely keeping him!

6

Eight Days a Week (when seven just can't contain the disasters befalling you)

OKAY, IT'S TRUE, I know very little about real science. I don't even know all that much about so-called junk science, despite the fact that I know a lot of junk. My knowledge of the stars leans heavily in the direction of astrology as opposed to astronomy. Even so, I don't know if there really is such a thing as a harmonic convergence or whether one occurred back in 1987, ushering in a new age of man, but I'll tell you one thing: I know a *dis*harmonic convergence when I see one, or more accurately live through one. There can be no explanation for the horrendous eight-day week I experienced other than the precise alignment of every single natural and supernatural force of destruction and chaos. This coalition of malevolence made Mercury in retrograde seem like child's play. Until that eight-day week, there had been, what, maybe, three other times in history when negative forces of this magnitude had coalesced with such devastating consequences: when Vesuvius buried Pompeii, when the potato famine struck Ireland and when Miley Cyrus discovered twerking.

As with most "perfect" storms, the individual elements of my maelstrom had been brewing for a period of time before reaching their cataclysmic crescendo and combining to rain down disaster on every square millimeter of my already thoroughly shaken life. One short phone call set the ball of destruction in motion. I put the receiver to my ear one September morning in 2004 to hear Dick's unexpected and unwelcome voice on the other end. A wave of nausea washed over me. Not once since he'd handed in his resignation from our marriage nearly two years earlier had a phone call from Dick ever brought good news, from finding out that he was going to leave me on the hook for tens of thousands of dollars more of his debt than he had originally disclosed to finding out that his new friends believed that I was dead. Since our divorce had been finalized in February, most of our phone conversations had consisted of his elaborate lies about having mailed the (inadequate) alimony check on time, which, of course, he had not. He knew I was completely dependent on that extra money just to get by and he delighted in still having the power to control me from beyond the grave, so to speak. If he found my tone of voice or turn of phrase the least bit unsatisfactory, he would delay the check even more. It was an exhausting and demoralizing cat-and-mouse game, one he well knew I had little skill or desire to play. So, my reaction of nausea upon hearing his voice on the phone was well-founded. Weak-kneed, I sat down on the edge of my bed and braced myself for the latest hit.

"Hey," said the voice on the other end with an incongruous casualness bordering on sociopathy, considering the seriousness of the blow he was about to deliver. "So, yeah," he continued, as if it were then end of a conversation instead of the introduction of one, "I'm not going to be paying you any more alimony. So, okay, yeah, that's it"

That was the extent of the conversation on his end—his greeting, message and explanation all rolled into one. He was ready to hang up, having dismissed the whole issue with a summary "that's it."

That's it? That's *it*? *That's it*? No siree, Bob, that most certainly was *not* it to me! It was not "that's it," as in this was a trivial little detail, requiring no discussion, and it certainly wasn't "that's it," as in this was a done deal with no recourse for me.

What it was, without question, was an out and out breach of a legally executed contract with definite prescribed legal ramifications.

Unlike quitting his job without telling me to start a business he knew nothing about, unlike liquidating all of our investments and emptying all our bank accounts to keep the waterlogged mess afloat for a few minutes longer, unlike running up my credit cards for $40,000 (including to pay for dinners with Honeypot), unlike hitting up my family for money—including my ex-brother-in-law—without my knowledge, *this* was not his choice to do; it was his legal obligation (he obviously had no notion of moral obligation). He had signed on the dotted line, agreeing to pay me alimony for a period of five years. To this point he had paid only eight months, all of which, as I said, had been significantly late.

And guess what? In the end, that really was it—just as he had known it would be, just as he had likely calculated it to be. During the divorce proceedings, he had insisted that he was minutes from declaring bankruptcy, which is why the attorney advised me to ask for alimony instead of a debt settlement, since alimony obligations could not be discharged in a bankruptcy. Even though the money he was to pay me over the next five years really was more of a debt settlement (a mere drop in the bucket compared to what he had lost of our shared funds), and even though I would take a tax hit and he would get a tax break, classifying the money as alimony was the safer bet with his bankruptcy filing looming on the horizon. And should Dick fail to meet his obligation to me, the attorney further explained, a judge would order his wages garnished...as long as he was still living in the state where the divorce took place. Ah, there was the rub, which I came to find out a little too late. Dick had left both his newly found job and the state about ten days before the alimony agreement went into effect. Coincidence, hmm. His residing out of state left me with two choices to make him honor his commitment—to pay an attorney a $10,000 retainer to pursue the matter for me or 2) pursue it myself, which entailed working through reciprocal state agreements and would likely take about a year to resolve. I had neither $10,000 nor time to spend pursuing it on my own, which he knew full well, so once again, I had no choice but to accept his terms. (P.S. He never did file for bankruptcy as he had insisted he'd have to do, so I took a tax hit and still ended up with next-to-nothing in the end!)

That call—which ended with him saying, "Hey, you want something from me, try to come and get it"—signaled the end of even the slightest, most precarious financial and emotional equilibrium I had managed to achieve in the eight months following my final divorce decree. I was just barely keeping my head above water, working two jobs, and had planned to hold onto the house for two more years to 1) allow Torrie to save money by living at home for a while after graduating from college and 2) allow me to finish the coursework I needed to qualify for a new, higher level teaching position, with said new position determining where I would move after selling the house. Living in our house was the sole constant for my daughter and me during this period of mass upheaval, the one area of our lives that was nailed down and settled, the one thing that we didn't have to fret over just yet. We had a plan, for crying out loud!

Obviously, our plan had just changed dramatically. By my calculations, I needed to sell my house within the next seven minutes, as well as take on a third job, if I wanted to buy groceries, so I had to postpone the heart attack that was threatening to strike me at that moment. With the help of a good friend, I found an able broker and agent and had my house listed by the end of the next day. Jorge immediately kicked into high gear to help me and began attending to a list of little things in the house that needed to be made buyer-ready. The house was only five years old, so there were no major issues, except for one—the French doors leading to a small terrace off the living room. These doors had been a source of tension from Day 1. They were not part of the original design, but Dick had *insisted* that they be put in. To be fair, he had virtually re-designed the entire house and it had turned out beautifully. (Character, he has none, but a great eye for design, that he definitely does have.) It was a sublimely cool house, and the living room as originally designed all but cried out for the addition of French doors and a stone terrace. Our builder, however, had put his foot down at the addition of French doors so late in the game, refusing to source them or redraw the plans to accommodate them. He wrote into our contract that he would take no responsibility for anything related to the installation or performance of said doors. So, Dick went out on his own and ran smack up against some mighty hefty prices—prohibitively so—for custom made French doors. Relentless once he gets an idea in head, Dick left no stone unturned in his search for a door deal and finally negotiated "a great bargain" with a supplier who looked as if he himself had crawled out from under one of the overturned stones. The doors were fabricated and installed and, truth be told, they really looked great! Until they didn't, by which time Dick had left not only the state, but also me holding the bag, yet again.

It's funny how things—French doors, marriages, what have you—go bad almost imperceptibly, little by little. Home maintenance had not been high on my priority list for several months even before Dick's departure, but sometime in between attending my father on his deathbed and discovering Dick was in Honeypot's bed, I had noticed that the much-debated doors "looked funny." Inspecting them more closely, I could see that one of them was beginning to warp a bit. As the builder had disowned them and the shady supplier had slithered back under his rock, fixing the doors fell to us, and by us, I mean Dick, and by Dick, I mean no one. I lacked the ability; he, the desire. He had apparently determined that there was no point in fixing doors he was secretly planning to run out of soon! All of which is to say that despite Dick's repeated promises to repair the poorly weather-proofed doors, their condition continued to deteriorate. By the time of the forced fire sale, one door was visibly warped and dragged against the floor a bit when opened. I was frantic. Dental floss strained my budget at that point; I certainly couldn't afford a new set of custom made French doors.

I pointed out the door situation to my realtor Mandy and she dismissed it as an easy fix. She asked me point blank if the doors leaked. I told her the absolute truth—no, not a drop of water had ever come in. Even I would have noticed that. She surmised that it was the combination of a poorly sealed door and Atlanta's humidity. Her thought was to take down the offending door, plane a little off the bottom so it didn't drag, and re-hang it.

"As long as it doesn't leak and it's only cosmetic, let's just let it be an issue for a buyer to raise as a point of negotiation, if it comes to that," she said matter-of-factly. Whew, an easy fix. I was so relieved. (Ah, the naiveté is touching in retrospect.)

Mandy was planning an open house for the following week to allow me time to get everything in tip-top shape. About seventeen minutes after the sign went up in front of the house, there was knock on my door. On my porch stood a very respectable-looking elderly couple, whom I failed to recognize at the time as Satan and his bride. Talk about a curse in disguise. When I opened the door, the husband wasted no time launching into what I now know is his doddering, slightly befuddled—and initially quite effective—*act*. This was his rehearsed m.o., intended to engender in me feelings of sympathy, compassion and any other emotions conducive to my giving them my house and all its contents for free. He asked if they could see the house. Uncertain exactly how to handle this situation, I hesitated and then asked if they were working with a realtor, and told them, if not, they could contact mine to set up an appointment. He responded, stumbling around, that they really didn't know how these things worked nowadays, as they had lived in their house for almost 40 years. Their home had too much land to keep up at their age, he continued, and in addition to the smaller and more level lots my neighborhood offered, they also liked its convenient location and security.

"We've been keeping an eye on this neighborhood," he said, "and houses don't come up for sale here very often. We are big fans of your builder, but we've never been inside any of the homes he has built here. Couldn't we just take a quick peek?" he all but pleaded.

I caved and let them in. What harm could it do to accommodate them, I thought, although I could already hear Mandy scolding me in my head. The quick peek lasted an hour, which was fully 59 minutes more than I needed to pronounce the husband to be the most annoying, grating, irritating, chew-your-leg-off-to-escape-from person who ever drew breath. As the wife stood stick-still with a stupefied expression on her face, he toddled about, inspecting and critiquing every nook and cranny of my house. For 60 excruciating minutes he bumbled, shuffled and prattled on, trying to wheedle out of me how low I would go on price and verbally cataloguing the many reasons why he would never pay more than X-number of dollars for this house (tens of thousands below not only the appraisal, but even well below my very attractive "quick sale" asking price). To hear him tell it, my extraordinary house was little better than a rat hole. His to-do list to bring the place up to snuff included such "improvements" as carpeting over the hardwood floors and tearing out the bluestone patio to pour a cement one. Given enough time, I'm sure he would have added boarding up the skylights, lowering the vaulted ceilings and squaring off the curved walls as well. This verbal desecration of my house was in addition to his repeatedly referring to me as a "divorcée" (what century was he in?) and his assumption that I must be "desperate to sell," (which, of course, I was, but I sure as hell wasn't going to let him know that) "without a man to take care of me." (News flash, golden-ager, a man is precisely why I'm in this desperate situation!). Meanwhile, the wife stared blankly with not so much as a single "harrumph" the entire length of their stay. By time they left, I wasn't sure who was more insane—the two of them, or me for granting them entry in the first place. I called Mandy and 'fessed up.

She gave me a stern talking-to, but in the end declined to officially write me up since it had been my first offense. I was grateful and promised not to pull such a stunt again. So, imagine my agitation when, the very next day, Lucifer showed up on my doorstep again. This time he had his daughter and son-in-law in tow and wanted me to let all three of them in for a tour. I wanted to scream, "Are you freaking kidding me?" Instead, I politely, but firmly, explained, as I had the day before, that he—or his realtor— needed to call my realtor and schedule an appointment. And this time I stuck to my guns, waving good-bye with exaggerated cheer and closing the door as the cloven-hoofed beast blathered on about "wanting just a peek," "having no realtor" and probably needing to take his pitchfork in for a tune-up, for all I know.

I had barely begun toasting my assertiveness when Mandy called to say Lucifer—who shall henceforth be referred to simply as Mr. G.—had called her to set up an appointment to see my house. He told her, as he had me, that he and his wife wanted to sell their home of 40 years to buy one that required less upkeep, was more conveniently located, blah, blah, blah...*and that they were not working with a real estate agent.* He kept her on the phone for more than half an hour, the entire time declaring his ignorance of the whole house-buying process since it had been years since he'd been through it. The bottom line, she told me, was that the whole famn damily—Ma, Pa, daughter and her hubby—was coming to see my house that very evening, so I cut my assertiveness celebration short and started polishing the toilet handles in preparation for the visitation.

Oh. My. Gawd. It was a demonic nightmare. Mandy said she had not seen anything like it in her 20 years in the business. She and I were outmaneuvered from the get-go. The "G's"—well, Pa, daughter and hubby, that is—came in guns a-blazing, their divide-and-conquer, take-no-prisoners strategy evident from the second their feet crossed my property line. They wasted no time with so much as a handshake or a howdy-do. They dumped old slow-moving Ma on the sofa and immediately started firing questions at us. Typical questions anyone would ask on a first home-viewing appointment—I wasn't counting their barging in on me off the street as an official viewing. You know, questions like, "Quick, tell me without looking, what are the model and reference numbers etched on the top and sides of the furnace capacitor?" "What is the name, address and phone number of the foundry where the iron railings for the fence two houses down were forged?" "What is the maiden name of the oldest living cousin on your father's mother's step-uncle's side?" They demanded—de-mand-ed, mind you— that I produce the plat map, original house blueprints and all appliance warranties. Mandy and I were at their beck and call for two solid hours, answering this, explaining that, going outside with one, upstairs with another and back around again and again. We fetched them iced tea, Kleenex and aspirin, for crying out loud. If my house had had a tail, they would have lifted it up and checked out the merchandise under there as well. All this while abandoned Ma sat motionless on the sofa. And all this before there was even a hint of an offer on the table. By the time they departed, lugging Ma to the car like a sack of potatoes, Mandy and I were too spent to do more than mutter a good night to each other. Our small shared comfort was that, if they did buy my house, Mandy would not have to split the commission since the G's had no realtor. If that were the case, she had already volunteered to lower her cut a percentage point to give me a break. We had both already more than earned a pay-off!

I picked up the phone the next morning to hear Mandy ask, "Well, guess who just called me?" When I offered the predictable response—Mr. G—she surprised me by saying, "No, even better...or worse, I guess is more accurate."

"What do you mean? Who called you?" I asked genuinely puzzled.

"Mr. G's real estate agent," she answered, enunciating each word with controlled rage. "Actually, I should say agents because it's a husband-and-wife team, and they want to present an offer to us."

"But there is no 'they,'" I shrieked. "We are the only 'they.' We did everything. There was never a single mention of any other agent. We both asked them that several times! You have more than earned the full commission on any offer the G-devils make. Can they do this to you?"

Mandy and I were seething. She and I had done all the heavy lifting and now two yahoos were going to waltz in and collect a commission check for nothing. When she told me the names of the other realtors, I screamed. I actually knew of them—I had dealt with them briefly when I was helping my sister look for a lot to build a new house.

"Oh, my gosh," I shrieked, "that's Big Hair and Bow Tie! No, we are not dealing with these people."

Big Hair and Bow Tie had been the listing agents on a few pieces of property that my sister was interested in seeing. How those two had ever built a successful career in real estate is beyond me, but I'm sure it was because they had deep roots in the community, a formerly rural area, as both of them had been born and raised on farms there and were related to nearly every person in the county. And possibly some of the livestock as well. Big Hair wore long, country print dresses and had her hair done up in a big, poofy Gibson Girl. She looked like she could have been one of the wives of a polygamist cult leader, which creeped me out right off the bat. Bow Tie looked like a cross between Bozo the Clown and Larry from the Three Stooges (with apologies to both) and topped off both his short sleeve button-up shirts and polo shirts with a clip-on plaid bow tie. They addressed each other as "Mother" and "Dad." In the short time that my sister and I dealt with them, they had revealed themselves to be impressively incompetent. They routinely got the appointment times wrong and left us sitting on the roadside for hours; once they sent us to the wrong address where we were greeted by a crazy old man who made up for what he lacked in front teeth with a shotgun and an aggressive goat. Their papers were disorganized, their information inaccurate and their grammar usage painful. Big Hair's response when we asked if she had any hint of new property coming on the market: "Well, nothing's camed up yet." There was no way we were dealing this couple, I reiterated to Mandy, on general principle and because it was too late for them to horn in on the deal now.

Mandy's broker was furious and placed a call to the Board of Realtors to investigate filing a formal complaint against BH and BT, but out of concern for my situation—that the G's might actually buy my house and that I needed to sell it as sooner rather than later—she held off taking any formal action. By that evening, I had the offer in my clenched-with-rage, insulted-beyond-words hands. Not only did they lowball it by almost $40,000 (when my asking price was already a full $50,000 below the appraisal), they wanted all the custom office furniture, the patio furniture, the stereo components, a TV, a

custom-designed light fixture (which was clearly excluded on my listing contract), all my area rugs (even though they said they were going
to put in carpeting?) *and* all my cookware because it looked nice on
the pot rack. Apparently, they didn't think my teeth looked nice in my
mouth or they surely would have asked for those too!

I am not opposed to anyone trying to get a good deal, but their
blatant and openly gleeful opportunism bordered on the sadistic.
Mandy calmed me down and helped me work out a counter-offer
for her to present the next morning. Although the next day was a
Saturday, I had to attend mandatory staff development for my job. My
boss, who knew my situation, graciously allowed me to keep my cell
phone out (on silent) and step out inconspicuously to answer Mandy's
call whenever it came. Uh, make that calls, very plural. I was up and
down from my seat, in and out of that auditorium, the caloric equiva-
lent of six brownie sundaes. Mandy presented my counter, which
clearly and firmly outlined *my* terms, and they countered—with all
the exact same conditions in their original offer while only coming
up in price about $1.25. Once again, I restated *my* counter offer—
emphasizing that there were two options, one price which included
the custom office furniture or a lower price that did not include the
furniture. I was not giving them $5,000 worth of furniture for nothing!
(I already had a buyer lined up who was salivating over this furniture.)
I also made it clear that the patio furniture, the stereo components,
the TV, the lighting fixture, the cookware, my padded bras and my eye
liner were not part of the house. I hoped that would bring negotiations
to a swift conclusion—yea or nay, I didn't really care anymore; I just
knew I was over these people and couldn't spend my day nickel-and-
diming back and forth with them. Ah, but it was not to be. My cell
phone vibrated every other minute for the next two hours, exhausting
my resolve and my boss's graciousness. Finally, during a break in our
training program, Mandy called to say we had reached an agreement.
It was still a bargain basement price, but Mandy was very concerned
that the sluggish sales market would only weaken more as we headed
into winter, so I finally accepted. She and I consoled ourselves with

the fact that at least those lying, cheating cheapskates weren't getting my office furniture! (Hey, you take comfort where you can.) Since all of the negotiating had taken place by phone, Mandy needed to get the actual contract from Big Hair and Bow Tie and bring it to my house for me to sign.

When Mandy arrived at my door, she was choking with rage. She thrust the contract at me, unable to speak. It stated the agreed-upon sales price, okay; a closing date three weeks hence, okay; and included all of the office furniture in the sale, huh? Their signatures were on it and the blank space next to my typed name seemed to be tapping its foot impatiently, waiting for me to sign. I was completely confused.

"What is this?" I asked. "This isn't the right contract, not the final one that I agreed to."

When she was able to speak, Mandy told me that when she went to retrieve the contract, this is what they gave her. When she told them exactly what I what I had just told her, that this was not the deal we had agreed to on the phone, all three of them, Big Hair, Bow tie and Lucifer (yes, back to referring to him in demonic terms) insisted that it was—knowing darn well it wasn't. She responded that I simply would not sign it because it was not the terms we had verbally negotiated, and they shamelessly replied that it was the word of three against one. With no other witnesses—the myriad calls were unfortunately not recorded for quality assurance—we were backed into a corner from which there were only two escape routes, give in or walk away. When Mandy said I would walk away, they said they would file a complaint against her and her broker for reneging on the deal. I felt like my head was going to explode. *They* were going to accuse *us* of chicanery and dirty-dealing? How could they even say that with straight faces? I had taken my first step through the looking glass into an upside down universe the night Dick nonchalantly stated, "I'm leaving" and, like Alice's world, mine had continued to grow curiouser and curiouser from that point on, but not in an amusing way. And as for me, I was growing furiouser and furiouser.

After much haranguing, head-banging and hand-wringing, once

again I was forced to capitulate, as carrying the full load of the mortgage (along with all the other debt that Dick had saddled me with) through the winter and possibly longer was more than I could do. I signed on the dotted line and told myself things would get better from that point on. Ha! I should have filed a complaint against myself for that blatant lie. I had given in to the Lucifers every inch of the way and had only one request, to delay the closing date by one week, so I could use my Thanksgiving break to pack up the house myself instead of paying the movers to do it. When I had agreed to close within three weeks, I was under the "mistaken" impression that I would have the money from selling my office furniture to offset my moving costs. Without that money, I would need to pack up the house myself, with the help of friends who generously volunteered to give me a hand. Asking for a one-week delay seemed a reasonable enough request. After all, they were not under the gun to move; they hadn't even put their house on the market yet. And, still, their answer was "no." They flat-out refused to budge even 24 hours, saying they absolutely needed to be in the house by Christmas and a one-week delay in closing would make that impossible. I had to borrow money from my mother to pay the extra $2,000 for packing services.

I had seventeen days to completely disassemble my life as I knew it, transport it to another, as yet unknown, location and reassemble it in some form or fashion. Seventeen days to find a new place to live, as well locate as a storage facility I could afford to stow all of the things that would not fit in an apartment, which was about 90% of my furnishings. I had already begun looking for an apartment, but was having difficulty finding a place that would accept 70-pound Jif, as well as provide enough green space for him. Most of the swankier new "apartment home communities" were not dog-friendly or their dog up-charge was beyond my budget. The ones that would affordably accept Jif were well below even his standards. The clock was ticking. I had seventeen days to pack up Torrie's room and all her belongings and get them moved to her new apartment. Seventeen days to leave a house I loved and move somewhere I most likely would not. Seventeen days to do everything without taking off any time from either of my two jobs. Of course, before any disassembling could begin, I—more specifically, my house—had to make it through the inspection that was scheduled for the next morning.

When the inspector for the Lucifers arrived, I was surprised at how normal and friendly he seemed. No pointed ears or tail. Hmmm, was it a ruse? He went through the house methodically, making notes, politely asking a few questions. When he went into the living room and neared the French doors, I held my breath and tried not to look nervous. Jorge had taken down the dragging door the week before, planed off the bottom, touched up the paint and re-hung it. The inspector looked the doors over more or less perfunctorily and moved on. I felt momentarily relieved, but knew I wouldn't really relax until I saw his written report. He faxed a copy to Mandy that afternoon and she came right over with it.

There was a short list of things he felt needed to be corrected and, which, of course, the buyers insisted I do or they would back out of the deal. The items were mainly piddly things, such as lubricating a window lock that was difficult to twist and adding a fresh bead of caulking in the guest bathroom. Amazingly, there was not even a mention of the French doors, much less any indication of concern about them. The inspector had, however, noticed a legitimate problem in the house that I had completely forgotten existed. When Dick and I had moved in the house five years earlier, we realized that the hot and cold water lines in the guest shower were reversed. We notified the builder at once, and continued to call and email him regularly about it, but he kept putting it off with a variety of excuses. After a while, we simply forgot about it—until our poor, unwitting guests would shriek in shock as ice water jolted them awake in their morning shower!

I spent every waking minute when not at work for the next few days nailing down details with my movers (and packers!), negotiating prices with storage facilities and looking for an acceptable apartment. Every should-have-been-but-wasn't sleeping minute, I spent sorting

the considerable contents of my house into four categories: to apartment, to storage, to garage sale, to trash. On the coming Saturday,
I had planned to hold a garage sale while Jorge took care of all the
inspection list items. He had already spent three days working like
a plow mule to clean up my extensive, but of late neglected, land-
scaping. As soon as the garage sale ended, I was scheduled to go
look at an apartment that would accept Jif. Jorge and I stayed up all
night Friday arranging and tagging all the items for the garage sale. At
7:00 a.m., I sent him to take a nap and I splashed water on my face,
brushed my teeth and readied myself for the early bird shoppers, the
ones who always showed up at least an hour before the official starting time. They didn't disappoint. As I was rinsing the toothpaste from
my mouth, Jif started barking furiously, signaling the arrival of my first
customers. There were no fewer than fifteen people standing in my
driveway, so I pressed the garage door switch and opened for business. With no one to help me man the sale, I ran at a frantic pace for
the next five hours, during which time Jif never once stopped barking
or racing from door to window, keeping himself fully apprised of who
was invading his domain, as well as putting every single invader on
notice that he was taking names and numbers.

Around 2:00 p.m., I finally got to go to the bathroom. Getting to
sit down for a minute, even on the toilet, felt like a luxury. I tried to
appreciate this respite because I knew the vultures would begin cir-
cling soon. As surely as the early birds descend to scoop up the best
merchandise in the pre-sale hours, the vultures swoop down in the
waning hours, hoping to pick your weary bones clean. Say the Hope
diamond somehow managed to go unsold during the first five hours
of your garage sale; the vultures, having scoped out the jewel incog-
nito earlier in the day, would show up at exactly three minutes before
closing and offer to take it off your hands for, oh, say, $12.50—and
act like they were doing you a big favor in the process. They count
on your exhaustion and desperation, as well as your desire not to
have to pack up all your stuff again, to close the deal. And, a lot of
times it works, especially with me, because I am more of a skilled

giver-awayer than a skilled seller. But maybe because I'd already lost so much, in so many ways, and was in the midst of losing yet more, this time I just refused to budge off my price of $.25 for an unopened bottle of OPI "The Thrill of Brazil" nail polish. The woman actually *countered* my "asking price" with an offer of a dime. Seriously? I stiffened my spine, threw back my shoulders and just said, "No." The Lucifers might have gotten the best of me and my house, but, by golly, I would not be robbed of my OPI nail polish! I lost the sale (she refused to come up to a quarter), but I regained my self-respect! Mandy later found out through a friend of a friend of a colleague that the Lucifers had actually sent a spy to my garage sale to see if I was selling anything that they wanted—and which they knew I would sell at a lower price to a stranger than I ever would to them. Their nefarious ways knew no bounds! I have no concrete proof, but I would have bet the house and office furniture I had already lost that the bargain-hunting manicurist was their plant. Vultures, all.

By the time I closed up shop for the day, Jorge, having completed all the other items on the inspector's list, was upstairs, attempting to fix the reversed water lines situation. Let me say first and foremost that Jorge is a civil engineer and is capable of fixing just about anything...with the now notable exception of my plumbing. Let me also say that Dick, who had been a construction executive, had lived with the plumbing situation for five years and never once attempted to fix it or so much as postulate about how to do it. It was my tacit understanding that he believed a plumber's expertise was needed. When I went inside the house, Jorge already had the wall around the shower faucet torn out and had wedged himself into about one square foot of space behind the bathroom wall to access the pipes. Walking into the bathroom, I was greeted with the sight of a debris-filled tub, as well as Jorge's arms jutting out through the opening in the wall. That was all I could see of him—flailing arms, no body. As unnerving as this sight was to me, it was at least ten times as much to Jif, who comes unglued if I sleep on the opposite side of the bed without notifying him in writing first. Routine is his life's blood. The day-long garage sale had already ratcheted up his anxiety to near meltdown level and seeing two seemingly disembodied arms poking out of the wall—accompanied by noisy banging on pipes—took him the rest of the way. Barking furiously, he ran in mad circles around and around the den adjacent to the bathroom, stopping only for a moment in response to the explosion of doggy diarrhea that unexpectedly shot out of him with the force of a fire hose.

I screamed, "Oh, my God, no! He has diarrhea!"

Jorge screamed, "What did you say?" from behind the wall.

I screamed back, "I said, 'He has diarrhea!'"

And then he screamed back at me "What? I can't understand you"

And so it went for several more unintelligible screams, while the whole time Jif continued expelling and tracking disgustingness over almost every inch of the formerly off-white carpet.

Jorge extricated himself from behind the bathroom wall, corralled Jif and was taking him outside to give him a bath when he yelled over his shoulder to me that he didn't have the necessary tools to fix the pipes, and that he'd already called a plumber, who was due to arrive any minute. I was spraying the 45th can of Lysol as the plumber ascended the stairs. I could be exaggerating, but I think the plumber declared the problem fixed before I even took the cap off the 46th can. I was going to be scrubbing dog diarrhea stains for at least two more nauseating hours and this guy had managed to earn $250 for about 37 seconds of work. Cha-ching, the sound of more money that I didn't have going down the properly plumbed drain.

In the middle of the clean-up operation, it dawned on me that I was scheduled to look at the "dog-friendly" apartment. I stopped scrubbing the carpet, disinfected myself and left Jorge to put the wall back together while I ran to meet the rental agent. All the way there I reminded myself repeatedly to keep quiet about why I was running late or rent negotiations would likely take a decidedly dog-unfriendly turn! I ended up renting the apartment, which was roughly the size of a contact lens case, though not nearly as charming, but which did boast a huge, dog-friendly backyard. Done deal.

All of this activity was the preamble to the "eight-day week" proper. The actual eight days began on the Wednesday following the weekend of doggy diarrhea and other plumbing malfunctions. I should have suspected trouble looming on the horizon, for as we all know, when it rains, it pours...specifically under my French doors and all over the living room floor, as I learned in Mandy's voice message during my lunch break.

The Lucifers, escorted by Big Hair and Bow Tie, had been scheduled to come by that day to take some wall measurements for furniture placement. At the last minute, some urgent matter prevented both the Lucifers and Big Hair from keeping the appointment. I don't know why—maybe Ma actually twitched or Big Hair had a hog-calling contest to attend, whatever—Bow Tie came by the house alone to get the requisite measurements on that very rainy morning. I guess this turn of events can be described as the sole stroke of good luck in a laughably-if-it-weren't-me protracted run of bad luck.

As Mandy related in the message, Bow Tie turned the corner into the living room and was forced to stop dead in his tracks, as the bridge was apparently out and he hadn't brought his waders. Okay, I exaggerate, but a stream of water was very obviously flowing from underneath the French doors and puddling up on the floor. Never in five years had one drop of water ever come in under the doors, not before they warped, not during the entire time they were warped or after the "quick fix" of their warping; never during the whole house inspection process had the issue of the doors ever been a concern, and now, five days from closing, water was flowing freely.

I can't imagine what would have happened if Lucifer had accompanied Bow Tie on this visit. Confronted with this situation alone, Bow Tie allowed his response to be guided solely by his ruling passion: greed. He was thinking of his commission check floating away when he called Mandy first instead of his clients. He told Mandy the situation and made this proposal: since he had been in the house a number of times on rainy days and had never seen a problem, he would give me until the pre-closing walk-through to remedy this "unusual" situation, during which time he would not mention anything about it to the Lucifers. He would come by early on the walk-through day and check the doors by spraying my garden hose directly on them. As long as the doors did not leak, the closing would go on. For once Bow Tie's lack of ethics benefitted me. Of course, the doors had to be fixed or, short of my buying a new pair of doors, the deal was likely dead in the water—or because of the water!

The clock was not merely ticking; it was pounding. I had to teach until 9:00 that night and had to be back in the classroom at 9:00 the next morning until 9:00 again that night, so nothing much would be accomplished until Friday, my day off. Not to mention, my movers were scheduled to pack up all my earthly possessions Thursday afternoon and all day Friday. As I blubbered my panic and disbelief about the doors—and cursed Dick all over again for getting them in the first place—Mandy tried to reassure me that she had a great "fix-it guy" who would come first thing Friday morning and work in and amongst the boxes and packing paper to make short order of this "unusual" leak. Friday morning dawned and Mr. Fix-it appeared, complete with tool box, multi-colored mohawk and what appeared to be full-body tattoos of various angry reptiles. He sized up the situation and dispatched me to Home Depot for about $40 worth of weather stripping, rubber door sweeps and I honestly don't remember what else any more. After about two hours and four trial sprays, water still streamed in under the left door and Mr. Fix-it gave up, told me I owed him $120 for his time and took off. My tears were giving the water under the door a run for its money at that point.

I waited until Jorge got out of work to call him and rant hysterically. As usual, he calmed me down and promised he would somehow make it okay. He and I worked on those freaking doors all Friday afternoon until midnight. We worked by porch light, spot light and flashlight. We filled every visible millimeter of space under the doors, between the doors, and around the doors with caulking, stripping or rubber stops. And each time we thought we had solved the problem, it was the same routine: 1) we would spray water on the doors to test them; 2) no water would come through the doors; 3) we would pre-maturely breathe a sigh of relief; 4) within 10 seconds, water would begin seeping in onto the floor. True, we were down to a seep from a stream, but it was still coming in. *But how? From where?* It was a big-ger mystery than where the WMD's had gone. With the movers due at 7:00 the next morning, we called it a night.

Saturday dawned cold and dreary, an omen, I thought. My move was actually two in one, with one load going to my apartment and the other to storage. My mover had a standing discount with a par-ticular storage facility, and while the location was not convenient to my new digs—the contact lens case—it was a good price for the large space I needed. I could have gotten by with a smaller space and saved several needed dollars if Torrie, 22 years old at the time, mind you, had agreed to part with even one-tenth of her childhood stuffed animals, all of whom were living in my attic rent free at the moment (and none of whom she had even thought about in at least the past ten years). When, in an uncharacteristic display of pragmatism over sentiment (desperate times, desperate measures), I asked if she would be willing to select a few special ones to keep and donate the rest to charity, she responded as if I had asked for both kidneys and a lobe of her liver.

"Mom, no!" she gasped in genuine shock and horror. "Those are my memories."

That was all she said and all she needed to say. In that brief ex-change, her recently acquired tough exterior betrayed her just a bit and I caught a glimpse of a long ago little girl, the one I had tucked into bed four thousand nights, the one forever tucked into my heart, the one who believed that the bunnies and bears—and the mommy and daddy who gave them to her—would always keep her safe from harm. And it broke my heart into more pieces than can be counted. I obviously couldn't make up for the mommy and daddy's broken promises, but I could make sure the boxed up bunnies and bears would be "there" for her, guardians of her memories, constant and true. And so 12 giant boxes full of freeloading fluffy toys headed to my storage unit and I reckoned the extra money they would siphon from my meager monthly budget well spent.

Shortly after noon, the movers had the apartment load on the truck and ready to go. Jorge and I led the way to my new home. We were there for two hours unloading and stacking and organizing. They set up my bed amidst the chaos, and after the movers left, I fell on the bare mattress and just cried and cried while Jorge sat patiently holding my hand. Everything I had sacrificed and worked for, dedicated myself to and believed in wholly without question for the past 24 years was gone. My family, my home, my long-delayed writing career, everything—gone, taken, stolen, and I had had no say in any of it. What remained was forever changed—my beliefs, my convictions, my values, all shaken and some exposed as hideously cruel lies. My easy and intimate relationship with my daughter, the heartbeat of my life, would never be the same. Her anger and hurt at being abandoned by her coward of a father were immense and crippling. If there is such a thing as the unpardonable sin, surely it is the conscious wounding of your own child to the core of her being. And surely one of most confounding mysteries of the universe is how the one who stays, the one who would never leave a child behind, bears the brunt of the havoc wrought by the one who walks out the door and never looks back. In the face of deep hurt, it is my nature to turn inward in sadness, and my daughter's to lash out in anger. Every bit of her anguish was directed outward, at the only target within her reach—me. As difficult as it was to be her whipping post, what was unbearable to me was that she had ever been hurt in such a way in the first place, especially by one she had trusted so completely. The one whose arms she had trusted to catch her when she jumped off the diving board for the first time. The one whose hands she had trusted to hold her steady the day the training wheels came off. The one who had reassured her time and again, "Don't worry, I've got you." How could he walk out on her, leave her without a dollar in her pocket or a roof over her head? How could he stand in my kitchen and wave away my pleading on her behalf by saying he simply didn't love her as much as I did? How could he leave her standing in the doorway of her bedroom, choking on sobs, his departing footsteps his only response to her plaintive cry, "Aren't I still important to you?" How could he do it? It would have been less painful for me if Dick had run over me in the street rather than hurt her this way. How could he?

After a fifteen-minute cry, I pulled myself together because not only was there still another, much larger load of furnishings waiting for my direction back at the house, but there was also the little matter of the still-leaky French doors. It was 7:00 p.m. by the time the movers pulled away from the house and Jorge and I were able to focus on the doors again. We spent the next 23.5 hours straight "examining" the doors—taking them down, resealing, repainting, re-hanging, everything short of putting them under a microscope. By 6:30 Sunday evening, we were out of aces and there was still water trickling in. It was at this point that I, untrained professional that I am, made the same observation that I had been making *for three days* (although this time at the top of my lungs)—that the water seemed to be coming from the under the metal threshold for the retractable screen and that perhaps we should just remove the whole thing. Dick had added the screen after the house had been built, and, once again, something that had at first seemed a great idea soured quickly. By the end of the first year, the screen panels no longer retracted smoothly; by the second year, the magnets failed to hold the two sides together when closed; by the third year, the screens were coming completely out of the frame and the thing was useless. (Hmm, sensing a theme yet?) At any rate, when I shouted my observation late on Sunday afternoon, I was merely expressing my frustration because I believed the two experts—Mr. Fix-it and Jorge--had already dismissed my theory. After all, when I had first made this observation to Mr. Fix-it, he completely ignored me as if I had never opened my mouth. I assumed it was because what I had said was so stupid that it didn't warrant a response. (Although I guess it's possible that hearing loss is a side effect of full-body tattooing.) I had also made the same observation to Jorge more than once, and he, too, had seemingly ignored me.

Again, I assumed his lack of response was due to his not wanting to embarrass me by pointing out the silliness of my remark. Well, guess what, folks? I, certainly no Mrs. Fix-it and definitely no civil engineer, was right all along! And it turned out that Jorge had not dismissed my observation as silly at all, but had fallen into the language gap that sometimes stood between us. He had no idea that the screen wasn't an integral part of the doors and that it was removable. He thought I had been lamenting the fact that the frame *couldn't* be removed. When I finally made him understand the situation, he couldn't get the screwdriver turning fast enough. The second the metal threshold broke contact with the brick, a torrent of water spilled out all over the terrace. Apparently, water had been collecting there every time it had rained for the past three years. Eventually the doors began absorbing the water through the screw holes, hence the saturation and warping. With the doors newly resealed and water-resistant, the pressure had built up until the water oozed out from under the threshold. And so, a mystery that could have been solved for free several days earlier was finally put to rest.

After disposing of the body (the screen and frame), we had to turn our attention to packing up the last things that we were moving by ourselves in a borrowed truck. I cannot remember why or how the heavy, unwieldy metal cabinet in the garage, packed to the gills, came to be one of those things, but it did. It's amazing how quickly the couple of things you leave to move by yourself multiply into a full truckload. It was equally amazing how little of the fully-packed metal cabinet's weight I was able to shoulder. I was close to useless in moving it, except for my repeated cries of "Oh, Jorge, be careful!" as if he hadn't thought of that himself. We finished loading up the truck and we headed off to the contact lens case under the cover of darkness, Jorge in the truck and me with Jif, following in my car. It was almost 11:00 p.m. when we began unloading, tracking and re-tracking a path from car and truck to apartment until all that was left was the beast of a cabinet. If I thought getting it onto the truck was dangerous, getting it off it was suicidal—for Jorge, that is, as once again my aid was limited to hysterical cries that he was going to kill himself. He loaded the ungainly behemoth onto his back and hauled it up a hill, across the expansive, dog-friendly yard and around to the storage unit in back. My legs buckled under me just watching him… and in anticipation of the 911 call I felt certain I would be making on his heart's behalf. Amazing me yet again, Jorge took it all in stride— one deliberate, carefully planted stride at a time, to be exact. It was just after midnight when he locked the door on the storage unit and we were exhausted and satisfied that we had done all we could do for one night. We planned to go inside, close our eyes to the chaos that surrounded us and catch a few hours of sleep for the first time in three days. Jif had other ideas.

As the diarrhea day had clearly illustrated, handling change with ease is not one of Jif's stronger traits. When we first got to the apartment, I took him inside, led him through maze of boxes and furniture and closed him in the bedroom so he would be safe while we unloaded. The result was not unlike twisting the hose faucet shut while the spigot it's connected to is still wide open. The pressure builds and builds…and then "thar she blows." In an unplanned, yet perfectly executed confluence of events, Jorge opened the front door a single heartbeat after I had opened the bedroom door, at which point Jif shot like a rocket out of the bedroom, down the stairs and out the front door, leaving us in a cloud of dust and dog hair. Of course, once we realized what that flash of brown that whizzed by us was, we immediately ran out the door after him. He was nowhere in sight, or at least not within the circle of lawn illuminated by the front porch light. We ran to the backyard, calling his name in panicked stage whispers, as it was now well past midnight and this wasn't exactly the introduction to the neighborhood I had planned.

We found a flashlight in the car and went to work tracking him down. I was terrified, thinking of the dangers that lurked in the dark, unfamiliar terrain for a frantic doggy. While he had done this—escaped the house and run with a compulsion bordering on lunacy— a few times when he was younger, that had been in a gated neighborhood that he knew—and where he was known! I was particularly afraid that he would find his way out onto the main road a few blocks away. We began driving up and down the streets of the "apartment community," with me hanging out the window, shining the flashlight, calling his name. I was certain someone would call the police on us. After a few passes around the area, I caught sight of a flash of brown lightning, shooting back and forth in the yards behind a row of townhouses. Jorge jerked the car to a stop and I leapt out to chase down lightning on four legs. Pure, unadulterated futility. Just as he had during the infamous cow pasture episode, Jif misread the situation as a game. If I chased him, he outran me; if I ran away and he chased me, he would stop just out of my reach of his collar. I had seen this routine before, so I finally accepted that we would just have to wait him out, wait until, exhausted, he came to the door step on his own. We set up camp on the little patio and watched him race back and forth...for almost *two hours*. I kept repeating a gender-corrected version of the prayer I had often recited during Torrie's unsanctioned teenage escapades—"Please, God, bring him home safely, so I can kill him myself." Completely bedraggled and panting like an asthmatic masher, he plopped himself down at our feet around 3:30 a.m. I was too tired to kill him.

Jorge had to leave for work in a little more than an hour, so he showered, dressed and fueled himself with high-test—100% Colombian, of course. I caught a couple hours of fitful sleep before going to work looking like death and unwittingly shod in one black and one brown flat. Funny side note: every woman, of every culture, saw my shoes, laughed and said, "Oh, no!" Every man, of every culture, had to be specifically directed to look at my shoes, at which point every one of them gave the same response, "What's the problem?"

My teaching schedule on Mondays was 9:00 a.m. to 3:30 p.m. and then 6:00 p.m. to 9:00 p.m. During the afternoon break on this particular Monday, I was not going home or running a few errands as usual, I was going to closing to hand over the keys to my beloved house, non-leaking French doors and all. I arrived at the attorney's office about 45 minutes early and went to the McDonald's across the street to get a diet Coke. It wasn't until I was standing in line at the counter, the grease-laden air clogging my nasal passages, that I realized I had not eaten in two days. The last meal I had had was a drive-thru lunch on Saturday somewhere between the house and the apartment. I determined I had earned the right to a McLean (they still made them in those days) and added that to my usual order of a large diet Coke. It was the quintessential fall day, bright yet crisp, and sitting there with my version of a Happy Meal, I felt almost hopeful, a feeling I nearly didn't recognize, as it had been absent for so long. I felt mildly optimistic, daring to believe for a moment that although this house ordeal had been a particularly horrific episode in the painful saga of my "new" life, maybe I had turned a corner, maybe things would start looking up from this low point on. Once again, the naiveté is amusing in retrospect.

I left MacDonald's and walked across the street—straight back into the bowels of hell, which I have now confirmed is any space occupied, even temporarily, by the Lucifers, or in this case even a single Lucifer, as the mister was flying solo at the closing, apparently confident that he could do without Ma's sage counsel. When I walked through the door of the closing attorney's office, I was immediately struck by the apparent lightness of the mood among Big Hair, Bow Tie and the Mister. The three of them were standing in the reception area, laughing and chatting together. They greeted me cheerily, as if welcoming me to a social gathering. Lucifer himself was downright chipper, a regular Mr. Congeniality. I felt I had crossed into an alternate reality.

"Well, now that the lovely lady is here, shall we?" he asked rhetorically, gesturing in the direction of the inner office, where Mandy and the closing attorney were already seated at the table. Who was this person and exactly how much ginko biloba had he ingested to regain mental acuity? Gone was the doddering, befuddled crank, replaced by this clear-headed, verbally facile smarm-meister. Both versions of him were equally repulsive to me.

When all was said and done, the lesson I took away from the closing table was that I was even more of an idiot than I had already believed myself to be. It turned out that Lucifer—you know, the old man who just couldn't understand how the whole confusing home-buying process worked, who couldn't complete a sentence without fumbling for every other word— was a minor real estate tycoon, having bought and sold at least five properties in the past several years, and was, in fact, the owner of a few rental properties around town. Additionally, it turned out that one of his biggest bargaining points during the negotiation phase—that he could do an all-cash deal if I agreed to a certain (lower) sales price—while, true, was not the whole story. Considering his newly revealed assets, paying the asking price for my house in cash even before selling his own very likely would not have "wiped him out financially," as he had previously (and repeatedly) purported the case to be.

"Who knows when or even if I'll be able to sell my house," had gone his "woe-is-me" refrain. "I'm leaving myself pretty vulnerable here, but a cash deal is a sure thing for you. No fear of the financing falling through at the last minute."

As I learned at the closing table, he had not even put his house up for sale yet and was considering holding onto it as a rental; therefore, it is highly improbable that paying a fair price for my house would have endangered the long-term health and well-being of either him or Ma. If "Ma" even was her real name! He probably rented her at "Stumps R Us" to play up the sympathy angle. Well, Ma—or whatever her real name was—may have been as dumb as a stump, but I would surely have to study years to even approach stump-level intelligence. Was there no end to my stupidity? And the cherry on top of it all was finding out that not only were they not planning to move into my house immediately, as they had said—necessitating my paying $2,000 more to have my house professionally packed up, as you may recall—they weren't moving until at least the end of January! More than two months away. I was livid...and completely impotent to do anything about it. It was an all too familiar sensation for me by then. After paying off the first mortgage, the second mortgage (taken out by Dick to finance part of his disastrous business venture), my mother, the movers, the security deposit for the storage facility, and the dog fee for my apartment, I walked away from the much-hyped cash deal with very little of said cash in my pocket. I wanted to throw up, but instead drove back to campus to teach my evening class. When I checked my voice mail at break, there was a message from Mandy saying she just had to tell me something now that the deal was done, something she had held back from me during the negotiations. Lucifer had told Big Hair and Bow Tie he wanted to add a condition to the sales contract—a provision, effective immediately and lasting until closing, requiring me to remove all my cookware from my pot rack so that I didn't accidentally drop a pot and crack the granite counter tops. He also wanted to request that I and anyone else who came in my house up until closing—in other words, while it was still *my* house—remove our shoes so that we didn't scratch the floors. The same hardwood floors, I point out once again, that he said, justifying a lowball price, they were going to have to carpet over. I'm surprised he didn't want me to use the bathroom at the gas station on the corner. Mandy had been right to hold that back from me. Thus ended Monday.

On Tuesdays, I taught at my regular school in the suburbs from 9:00 a.m. to 3:30 p.m. and then jumped in the car and drove 30 miles into the city to teach at another school from 5:00 p.m. to 7:00 p.m. The one small "victory" I had managed to wrangle out of Lucifer was to allow me to have access to the house for two days after closing—and, yes, I had to pay him two days' rent for the privilege. I needed the extra days to get a final few things that the movers had left behind, including the custom chandelier that Lucifer had originally wanted thrown into the deal for free. Too intimidated to take it down by himself, my mover had arranged for his "light fixture specialist" (really?) to come do it on moving day. The specialist, however, had gotten tied up (in electrical cord perhaps) and hadn't been able to make it that day. I was scheduled to meet him on Tuesday night after my evening class to take it down. "Access" to the house meant I still had to hand over my keys to Lucifer at closing, but that he would leave one inside a garage cabinet for me to use on Tuesday. I was to open the garage door with the code, get the key out of the cabinet and open the door into the house. Sounded simple enough, which should have been the tip-off, but my stumpness once again blocked the warning signal.

After my evening class on Tuesday, I drove the 30 miles back out to the suburbs through heavy rain and traffic, parked in the driveway, got out of the car, punched in the garage door code, walked into the garage and opened the cabinet—only to find that the key was not there. The door from the garage into the house was firmly locked. I walked around to the front and back doors just to be sure, but they, too, were locked securely. I was left standing empty-handed, on the outside looking in, a feeling I would experience all too often in the next several years. I retrieved my cell phone and called Mandy to ask if she could call Big Hair or Bow Tie and locate a key for me. I also called the light fixture specialist and told him of the slight glitch our plans had developed. He agreed to meet me as late as 9:00 p.m., for which I was immeasurably grateful. Mandy called me back to say she had only been able to leave a voice mail for Big Hair and Bow Tie. I really started to panic then because I could already envision how this whole thing would unfold:

1) I wouldn't be able to get into the house tonight, which would mean I would have to meet the lighting guy tomorrow, my last day with access to the house,
2) He could only meet in the morning the next day, at which time I would be teaching and would be unable to meet him,
3) It was too late now to get a sub for my morning class, so I would have to wait until the day after tomorrow,
4) I would, therefore, have to ask for one more day of house access,
5) Lucifer would certainly deny my request, as that would ensure that he would end up with my chandelier, which he had

wanted from the start and which was the one and only thing denied to him throughout this entire disastrous real estate transaction.

It was clear—I needed to get a key to the house that night! Suddenly, I remembered that Torrie had had an extra key at one point—maybe she still had it, I prayed. I called her immediately and, miracle of miracles, she not only still had it, she even knew where it was. Since she lived downtown, from whence I had just come, and since I needed to meet the light guy by 9:00 p.m., I asked if she could at least meet me halfway to make the drop. Of all the nights to need my daughter to do me a favor, it had to be this one.

"Aagghh," she exhaled in frustration, "why did you have to pick tonight? I have a date tonight."

Had she really just asked me why I had *picked* tonight, I thought? Well, gosh, tonight had just seemed the perfect night to be locked out of my ex-house. I had carefully considered all my options from every angle and had decided that tonight, after working all day and two hours into the evening, and driving back and forth in snarls of rain-drenched traffic, was *the* night for it. Wasn't tonight the obvious choice? I said none of that, of course.

"Can you meet me or not?" I asked in a carefully controlled tone of voice.

"Mom, no, I can't! I'm doing my hair!" she exclaimed.

"Maybe you don't understand. I'm locked out and I just drove 60 miles round-trip in a downpour and I don't have time to do it all over again. And I am not losing the chandelier to those horrible people," I begged.

"Mom, I don't have time. He's picking me up in half an hour," she whined.

"Can't you call him and explain, just start your date a little late?" I pleaded.

"He made reservations," she said. "And it's our first real date."

"And, again, can't you just call him and explain?" I repeated.

"No, I can't. I mean, you don't understand. He's really cool. I don't want him to think that I'm—"

"Think that you're what, considerate and thoughtful? Trust me, he won't," I snapped.

Not our finest moment. She finally agreed to "allow" me to drive the 30 miles back downtown to the restaurant where they were having dinner and get the key from her—as long as I didn't stay more than three seconds, speak one word or make eye contact. Weren't your children supposed to stop treating you like crap by her age? Apparently, mine had not gotten the memo. I jumped in the car and sped off into the rainy, foggy night with the clock ticking. The traffic in town was nightmarish, and my blood pressure inched upward as I inched my way along one of the city's main arteries. My battle against time was all but lost by the time I reached the packed parking lot of the persistently popular restaurant where they were dining. I cruised the dimly lit lot row by endless row, praying for a parking space, but there was not a single vacancy to be found. I could feel the chandelier slipping through my fingers as I made my third futile pass around the lot. Suddenly, through the shadowy mist, I spied an open space on the opposite side of the lot. I wended my way as expeditiously as possible in and out of the narrow lanes toward the opening, panicked that someone would beat me to it. When I was within inches of my target, I realized it wasn't really a parking space; it was a sort of access space to what appeared to be electrical and cable boxes. It was quite narrow, but I thought I could fit, and I hoped no one would need to access the utility boxes during the three minutes I estimated it would take me to go into the restaurant, get the key without making eye contact and return to my car. I gunned it into the space, squeezed my body out of my barely openable door and slithered through the two-inch space between my car and the adjacent one, whereupon I realized it was not the width that was the issue with this makeshift parking space, but the length. The utility boxes foreshortened it by a good two feet and the back end of my car was sticking out entirely too far. I was so frustrated and desperate that for a few seconds I actually debated leaving my car there and taking my chances. Finally, I decided that was just asking for trouble, especially with the falling rain and rising mist converging to blot out the sliver of light cast by the solitary lamp post. I sucked in my stomach as far as I could and contorted my way back into the driver's seat. I started the car, slipped it into reverse and…*smash, screech, crunch, thud*—take your pick of onomatopoetic words to describe the sound of my left rear fender making contact with something very solid. I slammed it into park and jumped out of my car to see—for the very first time—a three-foot-high yellow cement post, apparently put there to keep cars from driving too closely to some additional electrical boxes which I had also failed to see in the dark, until now. My jaw, stomach and heart all fell to the ground. I stood in the rain, trembling in disbelief at the sight before me. My rear fender was completely smashed in, with streaks of yellow paint deeply scored across its formerly flawless, white pearlescent surface. To add insult to injury, I heard a car engine start, and a space three cars away from where I was standing emptied. I took it and ran up the hill through the rain and entered the restaurant looking like a drowned, maniacal rat. I was sure Torrie would think I had done all of this on purpose just to embarrass her on her first date with Mr. Cool, but to my great shock, she not only apologized for not meeting me, but also offered to take the next day off and stay at our ex-house to meet the light fixture specialist since it was obvious I would not make it back there in time that night.

Wednesday passed in relative calm, and I taught all day and evening without a major catastrophe befalling me—although Torrie left me no fewer than seven voice messages throughout the day to report that she was variously a little cold (heat had been turned off), bored (no TV) or uncomfortable (no furniture) waiting at our ex-house for the specialist and the house cleaners to finish up. Seriously. What a hardship. My Thursday schedule was a repeat of Tuesday's, teach all day in the suburbs, drive into the city and teach my night class. The weather on this particular Thursday was a repeat of Tuesday's as well, pea-soup foggy and raining. I taught my day classes, drove into town and taught my night class and headed home, anticipating yet another grueling commute through rainy rush hour traffic on the web of interstates that define metro Atlanta. I had no clue what awaited me outside the classroom door.

I had been crawling along in more-stop-than-go traffic for almost an hour and was about halfway home. (This is a trip that takes about 35 minutes in light traffic, which, obviously, this was not.) As impatient as I was, and as tempting as it was to do, I knew better than to punch the accelerator during the occasional breaks in the otherwise gridlocked lanes. Flooring it when one or two car lengths of space suddenly opened in front of me inevitably meant slamming on the brakes a few seconds later—and perhaps not in time to avoid disaster. Apparently, not every driver in the northbound lanes of I-85 this particular evening understood this principle as well as I. Certainly not the elderly gentleman who, failing to slam on his brakes quickly enough, rear-ended me and caused a three-car pile-up behind us, just before Exit 103. I could not even believe it had happened. One second I was screaming in frustration, "Go!" at the string of red tail lights ahead of me and the very next I was screaming in panic, "Stop!" at the fast-approaching white headlights in my rearview mirror. Neither scream was effective; the traffic ahead did not advance and the car behind me most certainly did not stop. *Bam!* For the second time in as many days, I felt and heard the sickening thud of my car making unwanted contact with another solid object. While Monday's collision had been upsetting, it had not posed any great risk to my physical safety. The interstate collision was a different matter. Two lanes of heavy traffic hemmed me in on both sides (I'm so middle of the road), making it impossible for me to move to the relative safety of the shoulder. I was stuck there and was terrified that other drivers coming upon our pile-up unexpectedly would also be bad brake-slammers and ram us all again, possibly into the other lanes of traffic. I grabbed for my cell phone, which had been "blooping" its low battery warning for the past half hour, to call 911. The remaining charge lasted long enough for me to give the operator my information. She told me to stay put—like I had a choice—until the rescue vehicle arrived to safely escort us all to the side of the road. Just as I was hanging up from the call, there was a loud pounding on my window. I turned to see the elderly man who had hit me standing there, wobbling within inches of passing traffic (oh, sure, *now* it was practically whizzing by) and gesturing for me to put my window down. He was very shaken and rambled on apologetically, and I didn't mean to cut him short, but I was afraid he was going to get run over on the spot. I told him I had called 911 and begged him to get back in his car and just wait there. He continued to talk for a moment, but finally made his way back to his car and stayed put. Thank God, as the only way the night could have gotten any worse was if he'd been hit by a car while trying to apologize to me. I picked up my phone again to call Jorge, but by then the battery had gone completely dead. I envied it.

The emergency vehicle arrived after about 45 minutes and escorted all four cars off to the side of the road. The aid officer instructed us to stay in our cars and wait for the police to arrive, which they did about an hour later. And it was another half-hour before the police finished all the documentation and dismissed us to go our separate ways. It was 9:15 p.m. when I pulled back onto the interstate and nervously made my way home, arriving at 9:30 p.m., about an hour-and-a-half late. I was certain Jorge would be frantic about what had happened to me. I opened the door and quite unexpectedly ran smack into my washer and dryer (enough with the collisions already) which were, for some reason, sitting in the middle of the hallway. Startled, I let out a yelp, and equally startled, Jorge yelped because he hadn't heard me open the door from his position deep inside the laundry closet. He came crawling out and scrambled to his feet. All the words tumbled out of both of us at the same time: where were you, what happened, you have no idea what happened to me, etc. Somewhere in there, it hit me that I was hungry. Not only had I obviously not eaten dinner yet, I realized I had never had lunch. Jorge was clucking over me like a mother hen, reeling off a list of entrees he was prepared to whip up for me. I wanted one thing and one thing only and I didn't have much time to spare to get it.

"I want ice cream. That's all I want. I don't want soup or a sandwich or pheasant under glass," I said definitively. Publix was one mile from our doorstep and it closed at 10:00 p.m. "I just need you to drive me up to Publix right now before it closes because I really can't get behind the wheel again tonight." I felt I had earned the right to be unreasonable beyond reproach.

"Let's go," Jorge replied and off we went in his unwrecked car.

We walked inside Publix at 9:50 and went straight to the ice cream freezer. I grabbed a ½ gallon (which nowadays is really only 1.5 quarts or 1.42 liters, if you want to get metric about it) of Breyer's vanilla, paid for it and we got back in the car. Sometime in transit, I found out why the washer and dryer were in the middle of the hall. Jorge had gone straight to the apartment from work to get them set up for me, but the connection in the apartment didn't fit my washer, and he'd had to go to Home Depot and get 906 things to make it work, and, long story short, something that was supposed to be simple turned into a complicated hassle. Big shock there.

I didn't care if I ever did laundry again at that point. I would have agreed to wear dirty underwear for the rest of my natural life if it meant I could just go home, eat my ice cream—all of my ice cream—and go to bed. We slammed our car doors shut and put on our seat belts. Jorge put the key in the ignition, turned it and…and…and… nothing. Absolutely nothing. Not a whine or a whimper. Just nothing. His car, which had never ever in four years failed to start, failed to start. It was as dead as a door nail. In the middle of the Publix parking lot. At 10:15 at night. In the rain. After everything else in sight had closed. On a night when I had been rear-ended on the interstate. We could do nothing more than look at each other blankly. Could all of this really be happening? I picked up Jorge's cell phone and called Triple A whereupon I was informed that, while we would be rescued, we would need to pay a fairly hefty tow charge, as all of my free tows for the year had already been used up by my perennially breaking-down car. Fine, whatever, I thought, as I refocused on the critical matter of the 1.5 quart/1.42 liter container of ice cream beginning to melt on my lap. I was not about to miss out on my ice cream on top of everything else. It was akin to refusing to sell the bottle of nail polish for less than a quarter at my garage sale. I had to draw the line of surrender somewhere!

"There is nothing for us to do but sit here and wait for Triple A," I announced, "so, I intend to have my ice cream."

"How are you going to eat it if you don't have a spoon?" Jorge asked.

I began rooting around in my purse, my coat pockets, the glove compartment, anywhere a stray drive-thru spoon may been have been stowed for emergency use.

"Oh, that's just great," I huffed in disgust. "Five straws, two wrinkled Wendy's napkins and not one stinking spoon. This is the real tragedy here,"

"I'm sorry, baby," Jorge said sincerely. "We can buy more ice cream tomorrow."

"Oh, no, *señor*," I declared resolutely. "I am eating *this* ice cream, right here, right now. There is no tomorrow about it!"

"Honey, what are you going to do? You can't eat it with your fingers." Jorge declared, with more than a hint of pleading in his voice.

"No kidding, I am more creative than that," I snapped, as I rifled through my purse once again, this time pulling out my wallet and a sani-wipe.

"What are you doing?" Jorge asked, his voice rising in concern.

"Watch and learn, *hombre*," I said as I tore open the sani-wipe packet and pulled a credit card out of my wallet. I wiped off the plastic card, ripped the lid off the Breyers, peeled back the cellophane liner underneath and dug a rut right down the middle of the vanilla deliciousness with my credit card. My credit cards had long ago become useless for any other purpose, Dick had seen to that quite effectively.

"You are not going to—" Jorge began.

I tilted my head back and held the glop-laden rectangle of plastic at a 45-degree angle to my open mouth. The messy, melting confection slid right onto my tongue. Ah, sweet rush of victory! I savored every second of the cold, smooth sensation slipping across my tongue and down my throat. I don't know that I had ever seen Jorge look so horrified. I don't know that I had ever felt so gratified.

I would end up pitching the leaking carton of vanilla soup before getting anywhere near the end of it. The tow truck would eventually arrive and haul Jorge's car to the Nissan dealership. We would once again get to bed very late and wake up exhausted the next day. We would have to pay for our respective car repairs, and so much more in the coming weeks and months, but for those few sweet moments in the car, late in the evening of Day 8, I felt victorious, in control of my destiny. The ill winds of fate had once again come banging on my door, and I had answered their call and prevailed. I had had my ice cream and eaten it too, even if I had had to put it on credit, so to speak.

Thus passed the eight-day week of my mercilessly disharmonic convergence. If Mercury in retrograde is the worst celestial fate that ever befalls you, well, all I can say is, thank your lucky stars!

7

My Funny Valentine

DICK FILED FOR divorce on December 13, 2003, which I took as a sign that we were probably not going to get back together. When the divorce was finalized on February 12, 2004, the chances for reconciliation seemed even more remote. His secretly marrying Honeypot sometime in the summer of 2004—although they divorced a few years later, big shock—pretty much nailed that door shut once and for all. I'm joking, but I do think both Jorge and I felt more relaxed with each succeeding step Dick took out of our lives. His reneging on the alimony agreement had put a crippling financial burden on me, but on the plus side, I was able to totally disengage from him four years sooner. (If only his creditors would get the message, as I am still hounded with calls from collection agencies trying to locate him, ten years after our divorce.) By February 2005, Jorge and I were quite seriously involved, and I started thinking that there might be a proposal coming my way on Valentine's Day. I started cooking up romantic plans as my gift to Jorge, plans which would also lend themselves nicely to any questions that needed to be popped.

The botanical garden was planning a perfectly dreamy event for the Saturday night preceding Valentine's Day—February 14th fell on a Monday that year. "Valentines in the Garden" featured a candlelight tour of an elaborate orchid exhibition, accompanied by romantic music, and capped off with dancing, drinks and dessert. Intoxicating fragrance, wine and candlelight—how could he not propose? Well, I found out how.

I had told Jorge that the whole evening was my Valentine's gift to him. I figured if he was about to give me a very expensive diamond ring, the least I could do was spring for dinner and the orchid tour! I was quite excited about the perfect night I had planned. Even the weather was cooperating, as the forecast called for a cool, clear evening with a bright, beautiful moon. Just perfect for a romantic garden stroll…and proposal. We started things off with dinner at a favorite restaurant. Now, I didn't expect the ring at dinner—that was what the moonlight later on was for—but, geez, I did expect *something*. Some flowers or candy, or, shoot, a piece of sugarless gum. Jorge, who gave me flowers for breathing, who wrote me long missives of love on his lunch hour, was completely empty-handed. When I gave him my card, he read it and said, "Oh, thank you, my love," and put it down on the table beside his plate. That was it. Not even a stinking card in return did he give me. Well, okay, I thought, he probably wants to wait and do everything on a moonlit path at the botanical garden. We finished dinner and headed off to our night of orchids and romance.

The event did not disappoint. If there were ever a setting for a marriage proposal, this was it. City lights glowing in the background. Soft moonlight spilling down among the trees. Lush, cascading orchids, perfuming the conservatory with their exotic fragrance. Not to mention, candlelit tables of decadently sumptuous desserts. This was romance with a capital "R." We strolled the paths, we sipped the wine, we swayed to the music, hell, we even fed each other the dang dessert—but we did not, I repeat, *did not*, get engaged. I couldn't even believe it. My perfectly planned evening had come to naught. No ring, no proposal, no nothing. By the time we got home, I had definitely lost that loving feeling.

By Monday, the actual Valentine's Day, I was over the whole stupid, Hallmark-manufactured holiday. I had to face my students, many of whom shared my suspicion that I would return to class with a ring on my finger. I headed everyone off at the pass by announcing at the beginning of every class, "You'll have to settle for having an engag-*ing* teacher because you sure don't have an engag*ed* one!" Mondays seem long and tiring for everyone, I'm sure, but for me they actually were especially long, as I taught from nine in the morning until nine at night. This Monday seemed particularly dreary after the disappoint-ing weekend and also because of the very strange weather system that had settled over the Atlanta area. A thick blanket of fog had started rolling in around noon, and all day at school we watched it through our classroom windows as it thickened, eventually obscuring even the trees that grew not two feet outside our glass front doors. Evening students arrived late, if at all, with tales of terrible traffic back-ups and multiple accidents due to the zero visibility. Television and radio stations were announcing travel advisories, and the state police were urging folks to stay off the road if at all possible. It was definitely treacherous going out there, and I was just looking forward to going home after this seemingly endless day, taking a hot shower and going to bed.

Shortly after 9:00 p.m., I opened the door to the teacher's parking lot and was shocked at how unbelievably thick the strange stew of fog and mist truly was. I couldn't even see the cars parked in the lot just steps away. Wow, I thought, I am even scared to drive the short distance home. For a moment I thought about calling Jorge and ask-ing him to come get me, but that would mean a two-way trip, creating more opportunities for an accident. I'll just go slowly and carefully, I decided. As I was cautiously making my way down the short stair-case, I heard a familiar voice say, "Hello, my darling." It was Jorge! Oh, he read my mind, I thought. Gee, how had he so badly missed my mental message on Saturday night? Walking closer, I saw the full picture. He was standing at his car door, elegantly clad in a suit and tie, a large spray of red roses in his arms.

"What the heck are you doing?" I asked, sincerely confused, and sounding much more annoyed than appreciative.

"Happy Valentine's Day, my darling," he said, handing me the roses and kissing me.

"But that was Saturday," I said.

"Saturday was not February 14th," he said, contradicting me.

"Yes, but the 14th this year is a workday, so we celebrated it on Saturday," I countered.

"Who is 'we'?" he asked. "Maybe you, *gringa*, but for me, Valentine's Day is February 14th. And now we are going to dinner to celebrate on the *real* day."

I was sure he was doing all of this now because he felt guilty about not doing anything on Saturday. Yes, I had been disappointed then, but I was over it now. Go out to dinner now? Was he kidding? The make-up I had applied thirteen hours ago had completely worn off, my hair was a frizz-fest and my feet were killing me, even in my "teacher shoes." For crying out loud, I had been teaching for twelve *hours* and had to be back at it early the next morning; I just wanted to go home.

"Honey, it's not necessary, really," I insisted. "Let's just go home. It's fine. I'm not mad about Saturday."

But he was deaf to my protestations. He put me in his car and sprang the really big surprise on me. We were not only going to dinner, we were driving downtown to dinner, a good 25 miles away, at 9:30 at night, through possibly the worst fog in the history of fogs. I reminded him that we were taking our lives in our hands every single one of those 25 miles, too. It was indescribably foggy. And nerve-wracking. Why couldn't he just accept that I wasn't mad about Saturday and turn around and go home? I was tired. Driving was dangerous. We both had to get up early the next morning. "Waaaaaaaaaa," I moaned, whined and complained the entire way.

Once we—thankfully—arrived at the restaurant in one piece, my mood did a 180. I was swept away by the music, the wine, the festive spirit of it all. We had a lovely dinner and I apologized for having been so cranky.

"You were absolutely right," I admitted to Jorge. "This was a great idea. So, we'll be a little tired tomorrow morning; so what, we'll survive."

Jorge said he was glad I had enjoyed the evening and then asked, "Do you want anything else?"

Totally full and satisfied, I answered without hesitation, "No, no. I'm full."

"Are you sure you don't want anything?" he repeated.

"Yes, I mean, no. I mean, yes, I'm sure and, no, I don't want anything else, honey," I replied with finality.

Jorge was quiet for a minute and then said, "You know, when you are speaking in Spanish, and someone asks if you want something, it is polite to ask the same thing in return," he instructed. "For example, if I say *'Quieres algo mas?'* to you, you should say, *'No, gracias, y tu?'"*

"Oh, *gracias* for the etiquette lesson, *señor*," I said, laughing. "All this for you to tell me you want to order coffee."

"Try again," he said, sounding like a task master. "Do you want anything else?"

"No, thank you," I replied dutifully. "And you?"

"Yes, I want to know if you will marry me," he said, pulling a little black box out of his jacket pocket and handing it to me.

I gasped first and then squealed. Oh, my gosh, he got me! He really, really got me! He hadn't screwed up on Saturday, after all. Monday evening wasn't the consolation prize; it was the main event, as he had planned it to be all along. When I opened the box, I really let out a squeal. The ring was spectacular, just like one we had looked at and I had mooned over. It is a rare occasion indeed that finds me speechless, but this was one. I was so thrilled, so delighted, so overwhelmed that I just kept clapping my hands together with excitement, kind of like a trained seal. Finally, I did kiss Jorge and accept his proposal. All the young couples seated around us figured out that the jig was up and started congratulating us, with the girls oohing and awing appropriately over my ring. What a sweet a couple we made, they all said, but I think they were secretly whispering, "Eww, old people kissing—disgusting!" And I'm sure all the guys were adding, "Buddy, if this is the way she dresses up for a night on the town *before* you're married, the future is not a pretty picture."

Finally, when everyone had stopped fussing over us, we got up and left the restaurant. Walking outside, we saw that the fog had started to lift.

"I don't think it will be as bad driving home," said Jorge.

"I'm not worried about it at all," I announced, "because I am not driving home."

"No?" asked Jorge. "Then how are you going to get home?"

"Honey," I said, pressing my cheek to his, "I am going to float the whole way there."

And seven years later, my feet still haven't quite touched down.

8

When Life Gives You Lemons, Make Lemonade—but what do you do with an Audi?

LET'S FACE IT—I know the truth about myself, so why pretend any longer? I might as well come clean and let the chips fall where they may. I am an addict, plain and simple. I am a pathetic and incurable connect-the-dots junkie, who lives only for those times when the disjointed pieces of life fit together and everything makes sense. Nothing is as exquisitely pleasurable for me as looking back and seeing how seemingly random events—often appearing to be disappointing dead-ends at the time—were merely detours on a much bigger map, necessary side trips that led me to my ultimate destination in wonderful and unforeseeable ways. I am hopelessly hooked on seeking meaning in every coincidence in life and I am not above inventing meaning where none obviously exists. My need to experience life as mysterious and magical is compulsive, and no matter how many times reality falls well below those expectations, I stubbornly and stupidly cling to the hope that the next time will be different. Forget a 12-step program; I fear even a 112-step program would not be enough to free me of this obsession.

And so, some years back, when a series of uncanny coincidences led Dick and me to an excellent deal from a private seller on the one and only car that I have ever admired—a pearlescent white Audi A4—and from one of which I had already willingly walked away because the dealer wouldn't come down in price, I agreed without the hesitation or trepidation that usually consumes me upon making a large cash expenditure. I had released that first Audi to the universe and a better one had come to me, so, in my mind—connect the dots—it obviously was meant to be.

We wrote the check on the spot, and it was mine free and clear. I, who know very little about cars and care even less, was simply over the moon about this particular one. Dick, who knows a lot about cars, thought it was a great purchase as well, a steal of a deal on an excellent car. For the first time in my life, I was psyched about an automobile, of all things. It was so snazzy, so zippy and, best of all, it had been ordained for me in the heavenlies, so I was assured of a smooth ride for the long haul. Or so I thought.

Even now, five years free of that hideous beast's stranglehold on my wallet, I can barely stand to think about the stacks of money I shoveled down its greedy gullet. It is painful enough to waste money when you have it, but wasting it when you have none to spare is the stuff strokes are made of. I have a folder jammed full of all the invoices, but I cannot bring myself to total them up and see the final sickening sum. I had planned to plunk that number down right here for shock value, so you could see just how outrageously wrong I was about this car having been divinely appointed for me—unless, of course, the divine plan had been for my complete ruination, in which case it was a smashing success. (And I have to say I have suspected that on more than one occasion.) The most I can bring myself to do is count the number of invoices—18. With figures like $850, $1,200, $2,300, and on and on, ad nauseum. Truly, I am "nauseumed." That "divinely appointed" car was bought and paid for all over again in repair costs. Were I to truthfully catalogue each breakdown episode here, the sheer number of them would strain the imagination, but I assure you each and every one happened, leaving me repeatedly stranded in strange and unfamiliar places, from deserted parking lots at night to lonely roadsides far from home to the middle of a congested intersection. Once the damn thing died on my way home from retrieving it at the dealer—where it had undergone another costly repair—in the drive-thru line at McDonald's. My original intention had been to get a diet Coke, but I definitely needed a fifth of rum to go with it by the time the tow truck came to haul the mechanical menace back to the dealer.

If you're thinking, "Why didn't she just get rid of the thing?" that is the painfully ironic twist here. Getting rid of it had been my intention from the instant I found out that Dick had poured every single penny of our money down the drain of his failed—additional note of irony here—automotive-related business. I had already incurred some costly repairs, seemingly out of sync with a nearly new car of a good pedigree, and had decided to sell it, buy something more economical and put the little profit I projected I would make away for the leaner days ahead. (At the time, I had no clue how lean and long those days would turn out to be!) In fact, the "For Sale" sign I bought a few months after Dick walked out is right now, almost nine years later, sitting on a shelf in my garage. I could actually sell the "For Sale" sign because it is like new. I was never able to use it because, as if sensing betrayal, the vengeful monster began making strange noises the very day I came home with the sign. I immediately took it to a nearby mechanic I'd met for what I hoped would be a quick fix and then I planned to slap the sign in the window ASAP. Unfortunately, there was no quick fix. The laundry list of items that the mechanic said needed to be addressed was far beyond my means, so I did $600 worth of what needed immediate attention to make is sellable.

"You'll get much more for it if you do these basic things now," the mechanic assured me.

I certainly wanted to get top dollar, but I also wanted to get that top dollar before I approached the tipping point where I had so much invested in it that selling it no longer made sense. I authorized the repairs and comforted myself with the thought of soon being able to sign the title over to someone else. I picked the car up on a Tuesday afternoon, ran a few errands, and stopped at QuikTrip for gas on the way home. And "stopped" would definitely be the operative word here. After I had filled up, I pulled into a parking space in front of the store to run in and get a drink. When I returned and attempted to start the car, it wouldn't. Start, that is. At all. Shaking in anger and disbelief, I banged out several cell phone calls—to Jorge to come get me, to the mechanic to tell him the car was NOT fixed, to Triple A to come haul the car back to the mechanic and to a friend to yet again beg a ride to work the next day. I sat in my very parked car, fuming for 45 minutes, until Triple A finally arrived. Jorge arrived shortly thereafter and when he and the Triple A driver pushed my car to position it to be loaded onto the flat bed, I jokingly said, "Watch it start now." It did. I couldn't even believe it. I was able to drive it to the mechanic, but I had already used up a Triple A call.

From that moment on, I became trapped in a vicious and financially devastating cycle of breakdowns and repairs. Each time I had the thing hauled in for another repair, the technicians—from two different dealerships as well as two independent mechanics— would tell me the same thing, "Well, you might as well keep it now because 1) you have invested a lot of money in it and 2) you have fixed everything big that could go wrong with it. And each time, my car seemed to take that as a challenge and would go out of its way to develop yet another inconceivable ailment, usually when I needed it most to come through for me. Coolant would mysteriously disappear within its bowels, smoke would suddenly begin pouring out from under the hood, new batteries died and fuses blew without provocation. It seemed to have a particular aversion to being driven to Florida, breaking down three times in as many trips between Georgia and Florida, causing me to 1) nearly miss my niece's wedding, 2) spend two full days of vacation in an automotive repair shop waiting room and 3) fear for my life in a darkened gas station parking lot at midnight.

In addition to the myriad of internal issues, my car developed a host of external problems as well, mainly as a result of the rear bumper having transformed into some kind of super magnet, attracting other cars to it with astonishing intensity—and frequency. Over the course of three years, I was rear-ended four times, not to mention sideswiped once, and I had a king-sized steel mattress frame dropped on my trunk door. It was beyond bizarre—and certainly flew in the face of my having believed the purchase of this car had been approved by God. It was as if this car had some kind of curse on it, and seeing me as a carrier, friends and colleagues alike began backing away from me for fear of catching it. My boss only half-jokingly warned others not to stand too close to me, people lit sage candles when I passed their desks and I even had a friend from Brazil offer to perform an exorcism of sorts on both me and my car. It was a tempting offer.

Breakdown by breakdown, that car drained my already anemic bank account down to single digits. And as if that wasn't bad enough, one day I actually had a guy stop me in the parking lot at Target to tell me that both his father and his best friend had the exact same car—year, make, model, color—and neither had ever had so much as a loose hose in four years.

"Man, don't you just love that car? Nothing ever goes wrong with it," he crowed.

I didn't know whether to scream or cry. When I told him of my experience with the "wundercar," he just shook his head in complete disbelief.

"Wow, you're kidding," he exhaled. "That's unbelievable. Geez, you must have gotten the one lemon in the whole bunch."

The singular lemon in the entire crop yield, just my luck. The cosmic wires must have gotten crossed and somehow the divine approval intended for my car had been conferred on everyone else's instead. I suppose I should have checked my VIN more carefully.

By the time I was finally able to trade in my car, it was worth very little. I was surprised to feel my relief at unloading it undercut by a sadness that went far beyond my disappointment at having seen my dream car turn into a nightmare. It felt like yet another loss—alongside my marriage, my family, my finances, my house, my career. Everything that had been born in such happiness, with such high hopes for the future, was gone. Nothing but dust remained. Why? What had I done wrong? Those are questions that will certainly drive you insane.

Trying desperately to pull me out of my ruminating funk, my friend suggested that, painful though it was to lose things, perhaps that was what was needed for me to make a clean start. That and possibly the Brazilian exorcism.

"It's as if you have to get rid of anything that your ex-husband 'gave' you because it has been corrupted," she explained. "Don't think of it as loss; think of it as purification."

I appreciated her attempt to put a positive spin on my situation, but if what she said were true—and there was certainly some evidence to suggest it!—what were the implications for Torrie and Jif?

"Yikes," I replied, only half jokingly, "will I have to be purified of them too?"

Thankfully, in the end, I was able to keep both my "contaminated" daughter and dog, as well as pick up a wonderful husband, two incredible stepsons and an assortment of new and improved in-laws along the way. I am grateful every minute of every day for the miraculous ways so many of the gaping holes in my life have been richly re-filled in the past few years. I take nothing and no one for granted and try to hold each blessing with an open palm, knowing too well that there are no guarantees in life and that what's here today may be gone tomorrow. Tomorrow could well find any one of us knocked to our knees or even flat on our backs. I know that surviving one crisis is no guarantee that others will not follow. I also know myself well enough now to believe that whatever comes my way in the future, I will dig deep and do everything I can to rebuild. And rebuild. And rebuild again, if necessary. And I know one more thing—this positive attitude business and high-minded philosophizing is all well and good, but just between you and me, I have pretty much lost my taste for lemonade.

9

Home Sweet Homicide

WITH THE POSSIBLE exception of my daughter during puberty, I can think of no other object of my intense love and admiration that has caused me more heartache than my house. Make that houses. I have had a love/hate relationship with each of the houses I have inhabited in my adulthood. I have loved them; they have often been hateful to me. Again, just like my relationship with my pubescent daughter. I have bought and sold six houses over the past 25 years and each one was harder to get into and out of than a pair of skinny jeans after Thanksgiving dinner.

What has made their resistance to me so hurtful is how much I have loved them. I am not an overly materialistic person. Despite my two X chromosomes, I am a not much of a shopper and have near zero tolerance for malls, a source of longstanding dismay among my female friends and relatives. I am not clothes, make-up or jewelry crazy. I have never been much into having "things." Or, more specifically, having things just for the sake of having them or having particular things because it was cool. That has never been me, and at 56, I am definitely not out to impress anyone with my things. That is not to say, however, that I don't have discretionary spending plans for my future lottery winnings because the truth is I do like me a good house. And by good, again, I don't necessarily mean big and expensive—in fact, the older I get, the less space I want to care for—but having a house is important to me. I am definitely not someone who views a house solely as a shelter from the rain.

Home ownership for me is reflective of the divergent sides of my personality. On the one hand, while no one would ever mistake me for an introvert, for all my sociability, I value my alone time as well. Some days, I can think of no more delicious activity than being alone in my house—surrounded by my things. For as much as I eschew having things simply for the sake of having them, I most certainly do like to be surrounded with "my" particular things, items that touch me, express something important to me or, often, are just fun. In that regard, a house for me is an intensely personal expression and extension of who I am and I take considerable delight in that representation. During my three-year incarceration in the contact lens case, I missed my "things," packed away in storage, terribly.

On the other hand, the social side of me cannot be happy sitting in my house alone every day, no matter how many beloved things surround me. My house is never so fully alive as when it is filled with people. I love to entertain other people in my home and when my house is full, my heart is as well. And, so, no matter how personal an expression my house may be, it must also be welcoming to guests.

You would think that such care and thoughtfulness extended in its direction would make any house welcome me with open arms or wish me well when it was time for me to go. Yes, you would think that and you would be dead wrong. Every house I have had has played excruciatingly hard to get and then, conversely, has held onto me with the strength of a deranged stalker when I wanted to leave. The nightmare house sale to the Lucifers in "Eight Days a Week" was an extreme case, but it was not by any means the only bad house relationship I have had, starting with the purchase of my very first house with Dick in Charleston, West Virginia, in 1987. There was the typical back and forth bargaining, and at one point the deal was dead in the water only to be revived a week later when the sellers called saying they had decided to take our "low" offer. And in retrospect, of course, it became clear that we had overpaid with our so-called low offer.

That's not such an unusual first home-buying experience.

Dick and I were young enough to be totally enamored of old houses and found the notion of restoring the character and charm of an old gem hopelessly romantic. 25 years later, I am experienced enough to know that notion is just hopeless, period. But in 1987, that shake shingle house with the stone-walled driveway won my heart and the vision of what it could be seduced my soul. We moved in and began tearing out walls with great gusto, anxious to free our diamond from the considerable rough clinging to it. What we hadn't counted on was that Dick would be assigned an out-of-state project and would spend almost every week and many week-ends far away from our construction site, i.e., our house. He would come home long enough to demolish another area and then take off again, leaving Torrie and me quite literally in the dust. (Foreshadowing I was, unfortunately, not sharp enough to decipher at the time.) We cordoned off the torn-up rooms with sheets to keep the plentiful construction dust somewhat contained and lived for an entire winter with a tiny portion of the kitchen and adjoining dining room as our only usable space downstairs. We pushed the dining room table against the wall and used it as a combination desk/entertainment center. We shoved the couch into a corner of the dining room and Torrie and I spent four months of evenings on the couch, dinner plates balanced on our laps, watching cartoons.

Almost the same instant that we completed a lovely new playroom/den in the basement, Dick accepted an unexpected job offer in another state. We zoomed through the rest of the renovations, just in time to move away and never get to live in the house finished. We had only invested so much time and money in that house in the first place because we had anticipated living in it for several years, so we took a substantial financial hit when we had to sell so soon. Not to mention, we had three sales contracts fall apart a week before the proposed closings, which caused us to lose out on the house we had wanted in our new location, suburban Chicago. Our first dream house left a seriously nightmarish mark on us, but we got back on the horse and forged ahead with home ownership for the second time.

Moving from an icy cold housing market to a sizzling hot one meant our dollars did not stretch very far and we had already missed out on the one decent house we could afford. Competition was fierce and it seemed that house listings evaporated the minute they came on the market. We were forced to rent an apartment and continue looking for a house. We finally found one, and although it needed a lot of work, we were relieved to know we would finally have a house... until the pre-closing walk-through revealed that the owner had pulled out the nice, "newish" kitchen appliances and replaced them with crappy, "oldish" ones! Of course, this was in violation of our sales contract, but we were over a barrel time-wise and after arguing back and forth through our respective real estate agents, we gave in just as I'm sure she had anticipated we would.

The renovations that this 102-year-old house needed made our first house's reconstruction seem like playing with Tinker Toys. Although we had to make rent and mortgage payments at the same time, we were grateful to have the apartment to live in while we spent every free moment for almost three months tearing out hideous "improvements" and restoring the house with some integrity. My fingers actually bled from pulling thousands of carpet staples out of century-old hardwood floors. It was not unusual for us to be working until 2 a.m., with Torrie still in her school clothes, sleeping in the corner, and Ruckus, our dog, variously sticking her whole head in a bucket of paint, knocking the bucket of paint over or throwing herself against a freshly painted wall, adding a lovely fur-textured finish to it.

In the end, the house was really cute. And we got to live in it finished for about seventeen seconds before Dick was transferred to yet another location, Atlanta. This time around, selling in a hot market, we hoped to recoup the expense of our labor and also to have buyers lined up around the block, as we'd had to do a year earlier when we had been the buyers. Right on both counts, yahoo! And then not. We did get a good price for our house—profit from which went much farther where we were moving—but not until we had been victimized by a serial deal killer. She, the murdering menace, put in an offer almost as soon as our agent finished pounding the "for sale" sign into the ground, and we were overjoyed. Once we had signed a contract, Dick and I flew to Atlanta and found a home. We were set to close on the sale of the old house and move into the new house within days of each other. Then, suddenly, a series of back-and-forth issues with our so-called buyer cropped up. First, she wanted to change the closing date, and then she began questioning the home inspector's report. She was bent on creating problems where the inspector strongly testified none existed—until, finally, the night before I was to fly to Atlanta and finalize color selections for the new house, we got a message that our buyer was walking on the deal. And the pièce de resistance was that she was arguing for a full refund of her earnest money, based on her insistence that the inspector's report—submitted by the inspector *she* had selected—was inaccurate. My first reaction was to try slitting my veins with a butter knife, and then I called our agent back. Our agent related that she had just learned, a little too late, that this woman was notorious for writing contracts on houses, stringing the sellers along for weeks or months on end and then bolting. She'd killed deals before and she'd likely kill again. Yes, we'd come face to face with a genuine serial deal killer. The back-up contract we had fell apart because the buyer's mother was supplying the down payment money on the condition that her daughter, the buyer, break up with a boyfriend the mother did not like. At that, the daughter balked and walked. We finally got a solid contract from a mentally stable couple and moved into our new house in Atlanta two months later than originally planned. Whew!

Despite the hassle of the two-month delay, moving into the new house was relatively pain-free. And when I say "new" house, I mean brand-spanking new because by this time I had determined it was infinitely easier to make a new house look charmingly aged than to make an aged house look updated and new. I seem to recall some heated discussions between Dick and the builder regarding soffit and fascia, but, in general, move-in was okay. Move-out was a different story.

Lots and lots of traffic came and went, producing no bites, until along came a couple who showed real interest. They arrived for their first visit unaccompanied by their realtor, but very much accompanied by their two young children, who were quite a distraction. Dick and I volunteered to entertain the kids so that the couple could focus on the house. This couple ended up staying at our house for *one hour* while we watched videos with their kids, played with them on the neighbor's swing set, and plied them with juice boxes and cookies. We were exhausted when they finally left, but felt pretty sure that an offer would be forthcoming. Wrong. Their agent told us they were not yet ready to make an offer, but they did want to come back and measure for furniture. That seemed an encouraging sign. They came back the following day, *with* the children again, and we entertained the children, *again*, while they measured rooms and debated furniture placement for more than 45 minutes. In all, they returned four times, staying for nearly an hour each time, with us entertaining and feeding their children each time. I could have constructed a summer house out of the empty juice boxes left in their wake. We were sure we were being used as a babysitting service whenever this couple needed a break and were going to refuse to let them return when, surprise, they actually put in a contract. Of course, it was ridiculously low, contained a host of ridiculously unreasonable demands, blah, blah, blah. We finally came to an agreement, giving in on most everything they wanted, of course, because we just needed to move on. (We did, however, refuse to adopt their juiced-up children.)

Two days before closing, the movers came and packed up our house. They returned at 7:00 a.m. the morning of our closing day to begin loading the truck. They were due to arrive at our new home in Chicago in seven days, by which time we would be there as well, ready to unpack and move into yet another house. Our closing was set for 3:00 p.m. on truck-loading day, and I got a call at 11:00 a.m. from our agent, saying the buyers wanted to know if they could delay the closing because—get this—they had driven by the house earlier that morning and they didn't think the lawn looked quite as green as it had a week ago. They were serious. Fortunately, this was not a legitimate reason to delay or cancel a closing and we did, in fact, close that afternoon. I was prepared to spray paint the lawn green if necessary. Dick went to his office and I returned to the house to finish up with the movers. When they slammed the door shut on the full trailer and pulled away, I breathed a huge sigh of relief. But before the champagne could be uncorked, I got another call, this time from Dick. He'd just gotten a message from Joan, our real estate agent in Chicago, telling him, incredibly, that a major snag had developed with the house we had under contract, the house we were set to close on in five short days, the house to which all of our earthly possessions were now en route.

"We lost the house," he said.

This information would not even process. "What?" I asked, confused and irritated. "What house?"

He related the information our agent had given him. Apparently, a dispute had surfaced about a boundary line. It involved a driveway, an encroachment of 18 inches and an expired easement, culminating in a title that was not clear for sale.

"So, we just lost that house," he concluded.

"Oh, my God, no! This can't be happening to us!" I screamed in disbelief.

"You lose your keys," I continued in a mad rant, "you lose your mind, you lose your *virginity*, but for the love of God, you do *not* lose a house!"

But we had lost it. We were officially homeless. In two different cities at the same time. We had seven days to buy a house in one of the tightest real estate markets in the United States. You had to line up just to get the chance to put in an offer, and the ensuing bidding wars were bloodbaths for the buyers. Joan was one of the absolute best realtors in Chicagoland, but I didn't know how even she could produce a house out of thin air. But, miraculously, she called us back around 9:00 that evening—we were staying in a hotel—saying she had gotten wind of a house that was coming on the market the very next morning. We knew the neighborhood and had missed out on a house there before, so we were very interested in this one. I had already determined that unless there were live cheetahs living in it, we would take it! To have half a chance of getting it, one of us needed to be first in line outside of the house when the property was "released." It was an insane market there at the time. If you were not at the front of the line, a buyer ahead of you would likely step in the door, write a contract on the spot and it would be a done deal. I was leaving the next day to go to Kentucky for the weekend where I had a book signing and some appearances scheduled. (Yes, I was promoting my book all over the country during this same summer!) That meant Dick was up at bat. He left in the middle of the night, caught a pre-dawn flight and arrived at the house early enough to be first. This also meant that I was agreeing to buy and live in a house I had never set foot in. I reiterated my cheetah concern, but otherwise, gave him the green light to do whatever it took to buy it.

Dick actually arrived in Chicago almost two hours before the official "release time," and he and Joan deposited themselves on the seller's doorstep, hoping to get a jump on the competition. The seller, communicating through her agent, refused to let them in early, so they waited. I was, of course, calling every ten seconds for updates. Several other buyers had also arrived in the time leading up to the official viewing time, but "my team" was still first. The anticipation was killing me. I had instructed Dick to call me the instant he finished touring the house and tell me if we were buying it or not. The appointed hour of 10:00 a.m. came, and I waited for word from several states away. And waited. And waited. At 10:45, I still hadn't heard a word. I couldn't stand it any longer and I called Dick to learn that we had just entered a whole new level of crazy.

Forget any of the crazy buyers and sellers we had encountered in transactions past. This woman was all the way out of her mind. When 10:00 a.m. arrived, she refused to let anyone in to tour the house. She had some sort of meltdown and said she couldn't bear the thought of strange people coming in her house and touching her things. She said she hadn't realized that selling her house would involve actually letting people come inside to see it. Her agent, Sue, was trying to talk her down from the ledge while more and more prospective buyers lined up outside. It was completely bizarre, and I don't know why I had expected anything less. Dick and Joan finally were admitted a little after 12 noon. What they found, and relayed in great detail to me, was both wonderful and terrible. It was, they said, a wonderful house, four-year-old construction built to blend in with a historic neighborhood, with fantastic features and a location to die for. And a smell that indicated something or someone had indeed died for it, or in it, to be more exact. You could overlook the hideous tea-kettle-and-jam-jar motif of the kitchen wallpaper; you could ignore the peach-and-powder-blue color scheme of the half bath; you could even look past the hideous brass dining room chandelier; but, that smell, how did you not notice that smell? Everything else could be redone, repainted and redecorated, except the smell—of three cats that had obviously been permitted to use all four floors of this lovely home as a litter box every day for the past four years. (Okay, at least they weren't cheetahs.) The once-gleaming oak floors on the entire first floor were stained with streaks of black from marinating in cat urine. The very pricy Berber carpeting throughout other areas actually squished underfoot, a giant sponge filled to capacity with cat pee. This loony bird of a woman had managed in four short years to desecrate nearly every square inch of a pretty fabulous place. The floors would all need to be sanded and refinished; the carpeting would all have to be replaced; wallpaper would have to be removed; and three of the four floors needed to be repainted. It would be a major undertaking, time- and money-consuming, so naturally we bought it. But, not before the loon gave us several near-fatal heart attacks. After filling me in on the details of the place, Dick and Joan put together an offer and presented it before even leaving the house. Sue took the offer and told them the loon would respond by 3:00 p.m. Well, 3:00 p.m. came and went, as did 4:00 p.m. and 5:00 p.m. We were all going out of our minds, me from hundreds of miles away. Finally,

Sue called Joan. Sue, too, had been going crazy because she had presented the offer to her client and had then left for a showing at another house. When she returned at 2:00 p.m. to craft the response to our offer, the loon was nowhere to be found. Numerous calls to her cell phone all afternoon had gone unanswered, Sue related. Finally, around 5:30 p.m., the loon answered Sue's call and said she had left town because she had felt "so overwhelmed" and needed to be alone to "process." She would not be returning until Monday, she told Sue, by which time our offer would have expired. We, including Sue, who was seeing a done deal slip through her fingers, were all ready to pull our hair out—and choke the loon with it!

I'll cut to the chase. By the time we arrived at the closing table, the sane people were completely exhausted and out of patience with this seller's ridiculous shenanigans, which were capped off for me by the following incident. After all the back-and-forth with this major nutball, after having driven 400 miles, after having camped out for three days in a very cramped hotel room with Dick, Torrie and Ruckus, I was in dire need of a fix to calm my jangled nerves before going into the closing attorney's office. I was in full "Moe-Larry-cheese" mode and ducked into a convenience store next door to self-medicate with a diet Coke and a Peppermint Patty, which also happened to represent the sum of my sustenance for the previous 24 hours. By the time I entered the conference room at the attorney's office, the tense attitude toward the seller was palpable—even Sue was obviously curt and clipped in conversation with her client. It was obvious that everyone normal just wanted to be finished with this business once and for all. I gave a very quick nod in the nutball's direction during the introductions and settled myself into my chair to drink my diet Coke and eat my coveted Peppermint Patty.

As I was unscrewing the bottle cap, this crazy woman squealed, "Oh, great idea! I love Peppermint Patties. I haven't had one in years." With that, she reached across the table, took my Peppermint Patty and ate it." Took it and ate it! *Oh, my God, who the does that? Who takes someone else's Peppermint Patty?*

We closed, spent the next four months living in chaos one more time, undoing all the horrible damage that had been done. We finished up right around Thanksgiving and it looked beautiful. I was so happy, living in a house I loved, in a city I loved even more, and starting a job as a magazine writer that was fun and exciting. It had been another rough transition, but in the end, it was very gratifying. And at 5:00 p.m. on January 5, Dick was fired from his job of eleven years. In relatively short order, he accepted an offer from another company, and we moved back to Atlanta in April and into the house that I would in time have to sacrifice to the Lucifers in "Eight Days a Week."

So, you can see what a glutton for punishment and how stupid for love I have been—regarding houses, not ex-husbands, that is, although I certainly understand your confusion. You may wonder why I hold houses in such high esteem when I have been so shabbily treated by them on the coming and going ends. That's certainly a legitimate question. I think my answer is the same as the lesson Dorothy learned on her journey through Oz: There's no place like home. I realize, of course, that, as cross-stitched samplers say, "A house is made of brick and stone but a home is made of love alone." I know well that a home can be an apartment, a tent, a hut or a cave, but still, maybe because it's such a part of the traditional "American dream," to me there is nothing that feels like "home" more than a house. Nothing else imparts the sense of permanence, of roots, of "mine-ness" that a house does. I drank the Kool-aid at a young age and its effects were potent and long-lasting. I take one look at a porch swing and imagine the late night conversations that take place there, hushed murmurs barely audible over a soundtrack of crickets chirping in time with squeak-squeak of the swing. I walk into an empty dining room and envision a table laden with silver serving pieces; I hear the wine glasses clinking together for a holiday toast, and the intoxicating aroma of cinnamon and cloves is so real to me I actually get woozy.

With such outsized romantic expectations, homeowner heartbreak is inevitable, but despite my rough entries and exits, all the magical moments that have transpired in the space between those book ends have been worth it. The only thing worse than the hassle of buying and selling a house is not having a house at all, and I learned that the hard way, by being forced out of mine. Three years after my banishment from home ownership, when Jorge and I had worked our way into a position to buy a house, I couldn't jump in fast enough. Visions of sugar plums madly danced in my head—I would again get to host holiday dinners!—blotting out all memories of home-buying heartaches past.

Late one October afternoon, Jorge and I were cruising through a neighborhood when I spotted a house for sale that I thought had already sold a month before. I called the agent on my cell phone from the car and learned that the deal had fallen apart at the last minute and the seller was in a bind because he had already moved into a new house. He'd just lowered the price of the house substantially, making this house a very good buy for the area. I had been watching this neighborhood for a while and knew the price was a good one. I felt the dangerous stirrings of new love, oxytocin levels rising and bathing my brain in commitment soup. It was thrilling and frightening. The agent told us to wait there and she would meet us in about twenty minutes. Jorge and I got out of the car and walked up to the house. A very cute house but, oh my, with some interesting features we hadn't noticed from the street, such as pepper plants growing right outside the front door. As we opened the gate and walked into the backyard, our jaws dropped to the ground. The expansive backyard had been converted into a farm. I do not mean a garden; I mean the north 40. There were *crops*, growing higher than my head, rows upon rows of unrecognizable crops. With an irrigation system. In a suburban Atlanta subdivision. I was sure this violated every zoning ordinance on the books, but as it couldn't be seen from the road, I guess the homeowner had gotten away with it. Jorge and I were speechless.

The agent arrived and we went inside the house. My stomach quivered with excitement with each step we took. Overlooking grievous decorating choices, I squeezed Jorge's hand and nervously whispered, "This house could really work!" It had good bones and within a few seconds I had all of my furnishings mentally arranged—of course, I also had the whole kitchen gutted, every room repainted and all new lighting fixtures installed! After we finished touring the house, we sat in the driveway discussing it. Despite my mounting giddiness, I tried to be level-headed about the pros and cons. The big pros were 1) price; 2) the amount of space in the configuration that we needed; 3) great yard for Jif—once the crops had been harvested, that is. The cons were 1) kitchen needed a complete redo—cabinets, counters, appliances, floor, lighting; 2) repainting and lighting changes in all rooms; 3) reclamation of the backyard.

Suddenly, I started to feel very panicky about taking the plunge again and I was looking to Jorge to be the voice of reason, almost hoping he would put the kibosh on this house because of all the work involved, hoping he would save me from myself. Instead, his response to every negative I outlined was, "No problem. I can do it." Repaint the entire interior? No problem. Gut and redo the entire kitchen? No problem. Add three more floors, an elevator, and an 18-hole golf course? No problem.

We dove into the home-buying pool with all four feet. The contract negotiations were very smooth (suspiciously so, given my past experiences), which I attributed to the fact that the seller just needed to get this extra mortgage off his back. He had only one stipulation—that we use a particular mortgage company. His agent explained that the last deal had fallen through at the very last minute when the prospective buyers couldn't get financing—they had lied about even applying for it—and the seller was understandably concerned about a repeat performance. He insisted that we use his friend's mortgage company, so that he would get a heads-up immediately if there were any problems. Whether that was the full story—whether the seller was going to get anything in return for steering business to his friend—we didn't know, but as long as the friend's financing options were competitive, we agreed. The next day, our banker called to tell us our bank had just implemented a new mortgage program for good customers, an incredible deal that saved us a significant amount in points, fees and interest. She felt certain we would be approved, but we would have to write a new sales contract, deleting the condition that we use a specific mortgage company. Well, the other shoe had finally fallen. I knew there could not be any way I would ever be able to buy a house without major a snag. What an ordeal. The buyer was furious at the agent, thinking she'd brought him another flaky couple; the finance guy was mad that he'd lose our business and was telling the seller we were not trustworthy; the real estate agent was trying desperately to save the deal because she was both the listing and selling agent, but was related to the finance guy; and our loan processor at the bank went out of town, delaying our approval. And I was crying because I had already planned on serving Christmas dinner in a real house for the first time in three years. In the end, after 10,417 frantic texts, emails and phone calls, the seller was convinced by our banker that we were legit, and we closed the deal late on a Friday afternoon in November. (We were so grateful that the seller hung in there with us, that for six years now, we have invited him over to take a share of the bounty produced by the many fruit trees he had planted in our backyard.)

Throughout the whole buying process, Jorge had remained, true to form, calm and positive. Likewise, I had remained true to form, stressed-out and negative! Once the keys were finally in our hands, however, my entire demeanor changed. Walking in the door of *our house*, I was filled with absolute exhilaration—an emotion I hadn't felt for so long that I barely recognized it. I was gushing about how this would look and how we'd put such-and-such here or there when I realized that Jorge had a somber look on his face and hadn't said a word.

"What's wrong?" I asked, a nervous edge in my voice. Had he just noticed a hazardous waste dump in the side yard?

"Wow, baby," he said turning his head almost 360 degrees, "there is a lot of work to do here."

"What?!" I screamed. "You were Mr. 'No problem' every time I said that."

"I know," he replied soberly, "but now I really have to do it."

And do it he did! He was a machine. He plowed through the stalks in the backyard and the rest of the to-do list with a vengeance. Our goal was to have the kitchen redone in time for Christmas dinner. The house would not be finished by any means, but what a thrill to have a full-sized kitchen to cook in again. We had it all timed like clockwork. Jorge completed the kitchen demo on the weekend before he left for Colombia for my stepson's wedding. (Sadly, I couldn't leave school during final exams if I wanted my job to be there when I returned.) The cabinets were due to be delivered while he was gone. When he returned, he had a friend lined up to help him install them. From there, the new counter tops, sink and appliances could go in. In the mean time, we had no kitchen sink and had to wash dishes in the bathroom. We had already given the old stove (which was still in good condition, but didn't match our new appliances) to a relative and were using a portable microwave—which was stowed on top of the old kitchen island that was now sitting in the middle of the sunroom, waiting to be broken down and hauled away. It was pretty much a disaster area, but we had more than a week to go before Christmas, and we had a *plan*!

Oh, what I could teach both mice and men about best-laid plans. Predictably, the cabinets didn't arrive when originally promised. It was Friday, the day Jorge was coming back home, and the cabinets were not sitting in my garage as planned. Jorge was getting in late that evening and he and his friend had planned to spend Saturday installing the cabinets. Once the cabinets were in, Jorge could proceed with putting the rest of the kitchen back together in time for Christmas. The friend would be at knocking on our door at 7:00 a.m. the next morning. I needed the cabinets! I called the supplier again. Good news: the cabinets had arrived at the warehouse. Bad news: they were not scheduled for delivery to my house until after 4:00 p.m. the next day. That would not work. The only way I could get them before then was to pick them up myself. Really? Me? Alone? In what, the back of my Grand Vitara?

Well, I was not about to let my Christmas dinner vision go down the drain without a fight, so I went after the cabinets. I rented a truck. I called friends and asked permission to press their muscular teenage son into service for $100. The cabinets came boxed, strapped together and shrink-wrapped into a tower. The warehouse guys fork-lifted the whole tower intact into the truck bed. I was slightly hysterical because I was sure we would be tempting the laws of physics to get this load home without it toppling over. The warehouse guys didn't share my concern.

"Nah, you'll be fine," they insisted, dismissing my concerns out of hand. "We tied it down."

Then they chuckled under their breath as we drove off, "Don't take any sharp corners, ha, ha."

Ha, ha indeed! What a scene—my friends' son and I, transporting the leaning tower of cabinets in a pick-up truck, crawling about 20 mph down the highway. But we made it! I still can't believe we didn't get pulled over by the police and issued a stream of citations. We got to my house, and it took forever and a lot of muscle to get the cabinets separated enough to unload and stack in my garage. They were incredibly heavy and cumbersome to handle. My arms and back were aching, but I just kept imagining how wonderful it would be to cook Christmas dinner *in my own kitchen*. And my teenage assistant more than earned his pay, and hefty tip, that night! We were both sweating and worn out by the time we finished stacking the last cabinet. Then I drove him home, returned the truck and got back to my house shortly before Jorge walked in the door from the airport. He couldn't believe what I had done to get the cabinets there. Neither could I.

I had to chaperone an early morning basketball game at school Saturday morning. When I left the house, the guys were busy unpacking the cabinets and snapping chalk lines on the wall. My new kitchen was being born! All through the game, the anticipation of seeing the progress was killing me. Finally, the game was over and I headed home, filled with excitement. I pulled in the driveway, jumped out of the car and raced into the house. And I came to a screeching halt. The kitchen was just as I had left it. Jorge was alone and on the phone. What was going on?

What was going on was that there was a cabinet missing from the order. It had not been left behind at the warehouse; it had never even been sent to the warehouse. The last line of our order had somehow been deleted, so the cabinet had not been included. And it was not just any old cabinet that we could do without until it arrived. It was the corner cabinet, which had to be installed first, upon which the placement of the rest of the cabinets depended. It wasn't even the upper corner cabinet. It was the lower corner cabinet, without which the counter top and sink could not be installed. Jorge hung up the phone and told me it would be three weeks until the missing cabinet would arrive. Two weeks past Christmas. I was crestfallen. And twenty minutes of crying and cursing didn't make me feel any better, nor did it solve the problem. I had to accept that my longed-for Christmas dinner was not going to happen. Another twenty minutes of crying and cursing, and I finally gave in and began making other plans.

Well, things started off fairly well on Christmas Eve. Jorge, Torrie and I had a lovely dinner at a charming and appropriately festive restaurant, went to church, came home and watched some Christmas specials on TV before going to bed. Christmas morning dawned and breakfast options were limited to what could be made in a microwave or toaster. We decided to go out for something heartier, more of a brunch to take us through an afternoon movie. You know how everyone complains about Christmas being too commercialized? Well, not commercialized enough to provide any breakfast or brunch options besides Waffle House on Christmas morning, let me tell you. We all decided it would not be overly depressing to eat Christmas breakfast at Waffle House if we viewed it as a sort of quirky tradition. Besides, we were hungry. So, we had our Waffle House breakfast, and it was fine. Then we went home and opened presents, after which we headed to a late afternoon movie. Perhaps it wasn't quite a Norman Rockwell Christmas, but it was fine. Until after the movie. We exited the movie close to dinner time and realized anew that we had no kitchen to make dinner in. We scoured the area and the Internet to find an open restaurant and found out that we had two options: Waffle House and Golden Corral. It was just too hideously depressing to imagine dinner at either establishment on a rainy Christmas evening. Our backs were against the wall and we had to come up with an idea. In the meantime, we needed gas, so we went to QuikTrip—where, yes, I succumbed to hunger pangs and bought our official Christmas dinner, a microwave pizza and ice cream. After dinner, I washed our three plates, three bowls and three spoons—all that was missing was Goldilocks—in the bathroom sink and decided I'd had all the Christmas 2007 I could stand. It was lights out for me. As I was drifting off to sleep, I heard Torrie, a notorious cheater and bad sport, arguing with Jorge about the rules of Chinese Checkers.

"What do you mean I can't make that move? What—is it against some kind of Colombian rule?" she asked defensively.

"How Colombian?" he responded. "These are *Chinese* Checkers. The rules are international. You are cheating in every language!" he responded.

I fell asleep with a smile on my face, the comfortable chatter of a "father-daughter" competition the best Christmas lullaby I could imagine.

And so another turbulent house entry was completed. And six years later—after countless hours of painting, sanding, dry walling and rewiring—I know it was worth every struggle. In these six short years, my new family has made a whole new album of precious memories—birthdays, anniversaries, baby showers, even Jorge's citizenship party! One evening after a family dinner, Torrie was getting ready to return to her apartment. She stood, back against the front door, surveying a house she had never lived in, and spoke the magic words. "Now," she said with a sigh, "with all your things in here, Mom, it feels like home."

And can there be any more important reason to have a house? I think not.

10

Goodbye, Mr. Jif

ONE SUNNY OCTOBER afternoon back in 1999, Dick and I were out running errands. Every turn he made was completely predictable, post office, bank, Home Depot, no surprises. No surprises, that is, until he made a left-hand turn instead of continuing straight down the highway on our way home. This unexpected change of course shook me from my reverie.

"What are you doing?" I asked. "Why are you turning in here?" He was pulling into the Sports Authority parking lot.

"I just want to see something," he said, rather cryptically.

"What?" I asked. "What do you need to see?"

"Just something," he said, continuing the mysterious tone.

I couldn't understand why such mystery was necessary just to go check out a pair of sneakers or sweat pants, so, knowing Dick's great penchant for secret spending sprees, I got very nervous. I was expecting him to inform me of some large and unnecessary purchase he'd already made, like a $5,000 home gym, which we were now going to retrieve. But instead of stopping in front of Sports Authority, he continued driving past it to the PetSmart at the other end of the parking lot. When he pulled into a space there, I was really confused because not only did we have no reason to go to a pet store, simply driving by it was an unwelcome reminder of the painful loss I had suffered some months earlier. The past December, my beloved eleven-year-old English Springer Spaniel Ruckus had reached the end of her time on earth. Multiple physical infirmities as well as mid-stage dementia had overtaken this sweet girl, and I'd had to make the excruciatingly difficult decision to end her suffering. Ruckus loved everyone in the family, but there was no mistaking that she was my girl. I used to tease Dick that he could learn a thing or two about devotion and adoration from her. (Little did I realize the irony in those words at the time.) When I worked at my desk, she slept not merely at my feet, but on top of them. When I walked to the mailbox at the end of our driveway, which took all of 25 seconds round-trip, she watched my every step through the glass front door and whimpered forlornly until I was back inside with her—at which point she never failed to deliver a knockdown greeting as if I'd been gone at sea for a year.

In her last days, this attachment was heartbreaking to witness. She became more and more dependent on me as dementia stole more and more of her memory. One day she stood motionless before the open kitchen door, completely confused about how to cross its threshold to go outside. She looked up at me pleadingly, and I gently led her over the threshold and out into the yard. It seemed I was the last remaining touchstone to all that had been familiar to her for the previous eleven years. She became agitated if she lost sight of me for even a few moments; to keep her calm, I'd even had to embrace an open door policy in the bathroom when she and I were home alone. In a matter of weeks, agitation gave way to full-blown panic and she could not tolerate being separated from me at all. She completely exhausted herself trailing me from room to room and floor to floor in our four-story house. It was useless to assure her that I would be right back—I could go down three flights of stairs and return faster than her stiff hips could lift her off the floor—because her fear of being without me would not allow her to wait. So, slowly up and down the stairs we went together. Sometimes she would need to stop and rest mid-flight and I would stop, too, and sit down on the step beside her, hugging her tightly and trying to soak her into my bones, all the while knowing our days together were growing fewer and fewer with every dawn. Our "stair time" was the very definition of bittersweet.

Even though by then her passing had been ten months and an interstate move ago, some days the pain of losing her still felt very fresh. I knew that I would eventually have another dog in my life, but I was not ready yet, and this was certainly not the time, as we were living in a no-pet apartment while our new house was being built—and we would be living there for two months longer than planned since our builder was running that much behind schedule. So, I could not imagine why on earth Dick was bringing our car to a stop in front of PetSmart this particular Saturday afternoon. When I asked him as much, he said that it was adoption day and that he just wanted to look at the dogs. I protested as loudly and vigorously as possible.

"How can you do this to me?" I asked incredulously. "It is bad enough seeing them when I know I can't take them all home, but today it's worse because I know I can't even save one of them. I am not getting out of the car. My heart cannot take this right now!"

As he always did to get his way, he wheedled and cajoled relentlessly until I finally gave in. Reluctantly, I strolled past the row of cages on the sidewalk and did my utmost to stay detached, averting the gaze of both the dogs and the volunteer workers. I was standing still, staring out across the parking lot, when Dick came up and all but shoved a caramel-colored ball of wiggle into my arms. It is a challenge to stay emotionally detached when a puppy's tongue is physically attached to your face and his teeth have a grip on your nose. Every face lick seemed to reach all the way into my heart and melt away some of my resolve. I knew I was nearing the point of no return, and so, with quite uncharacteristic discipline, I handed the wiggly-waggly pup back to Dick and told him 1) we could not get a dog that day; 2) I would not be bullied into it; 3) he would be the one to tell the adoption coordinator because I was going back to the car.

I watched from the front seat of the car as Dick handed the puppy back to the coordinator, and I could see the coordinator nodding his head sympathetically as Dick explained that we were not taking the dog. Still nodding in agreement, the coordinator looked over at me in the car and mouthed the words, "I understand." I breathed a sigh of relief at my narrow escape. And then, still holding the dog in his arms, the coordinator—manipulative genius—took the puppy's right front paw in his hand and waved "bye-bye" to me.

Talk about your strong paw sales tactics. What choice did I have after that? None, obviously. I got out of the car and, resigned to my fate, walked back to the sidewalk where my new dog was being held.

"Put him in the car," I said.

"Pardon me?" the coordinator asked with fake innocence.

"You know darn well you heard me—put him in the car," I repeated.

I took the squirmy-wormy fur ball with me to the car while Dick filled out all the paperwork and paid the adoption fee.

And that is how my peanut butter puppy Jif—so named by me because, after all, choosy mothers choose Jif—moved in and set up housekeeping in my heart for a twelve-year run. From the get-go, it was apparent that life with Jif was going to be an adventure. First off, I had to smuggle him in and out of the "apartment community" where we were living while our house was being very slowly built. Pets were not prohibited in the community at large, but we were in a no-pet building and were not about to move to another building for the remaining two months of our stay. Fortunately, our building was near the back of the complex, a good distance from the management office, and all of the neighbors were in cahoots with us, declaring Jif the cutest thing this side of *101 Dalmatians*. The real challenge came every morning when I drove the two of us to the park to play. Invariably, someone official would be prowling around near the exit gate every time I drove out. It was as if an alarm sounded when I got in my car, alerting one of the rental agents to go stand there. Each day I had to arrange Jif on the floor on the passenger side of my car, hold him in place with my right hand and drive with the left, all the while smiling and nodding a greeting to the rental agent sentry. I was a nervous wreck worrying that at any moment I might lose my grip on him and his head would pop up like a jack-in-the-box, blowing our cover. I felt like I was on the old TV show *Hogan's Heroes*, trying to smuggle someone out past the Gestapo.

Once we moved into our new house, new challenges arose. It was obvious that I had not had a "baby" around for a long time and had completely forgotten how to properly puppy-proof a home. I carelessly left little things just lying around the house in plain sight. You know, little things, like the dining room chairs, the living room rug and the ottoman. I could hardly expect even the most disciplined puppy to resist taking a chomp or two—or twenty—out of such temptations; why, they had "chew toy" written all over them, and Jif turned out to be quite the proficient reader. In no time at all, the casualties numbered in the high double digits. In addition to the items above, it quickly grew to include seven fingers from a pair of leather gloves, one pair of men's sneakers, two pairs of women's dress shoes, three pairs of leggings, one pajama bottom, two sweat shirt sleeves, one fleece jacket, one winter coat, one down comforter, two cotton blankets, one duvet cover, the corner of a very nice table, a friend's potholder and dish towel and three, yes three, "indestructible" dog beds that obviously weren't. The chewing would prove to be a very difficult habit to break—they don't make a patch for that—and before it was brought under control would further claim as some of its most memorable victims a tax refund check, a pineapple upside down cake meant for company and a pricey wedge of Fontina cheese, stolen right off the serving tray in the middle of a dinner party. Although, in all fairness, Jif didn't steal the Fontina; he traded up for it. While my guests were, thankfully, eating dinner on the patio, I ducked into the house to retrieve another bottle of wine and caught Jif, cheese in mouth, running from the living room. In the middle of the serving tray on the coffee table, the spot the Fontina had formerly occupied, sat his partially chewed rawhide bone. Hey, you can't fault a dog for taking advantage of a good deal when it presents itself!

I never did tally up the final body count when all had been chewed and done, but the total wouldn't have mattered to me anyway. The unraveled threads Jif left in his wake were a small price to pay for the magical way he stitched up the ragged fibers of my heart. Jif's infectious *joie de vivre*—he was appropriately dubbed "Jif the Exuberant" by my friend Marilyn—picked up where antidepressants left off and dispersed the last shadows of my grief. He allowed me to keep my memories of Ruckus close to my heart without being devastated by them. So thoroughly did Jif re-ignite my own joy of living that a story about him, which I titled "Puppy Love," all but wrote itself. It was not only the easiest piece I had ever written, it was also one of the best. At the time, I was living in a kind of magic bubble where every word I committed to paper seemed to be picked up by some publication, somewhere, often leading to TV appearances or speaking invitations, so I was eagerly anticipating "Puppy Love" to make a big impact. My publicist (this was before of the days of blogging and do-it-yourself publishing) released the story to our regular outlets, as well as to several targeted "dog" publications, and we both sat back and waited for the overwhelming response…which never came. An underwhelming response never even came. Nothing ever came and continued not coming each time we re-sent the story over the next few months. We were both shocked and confounded.

"You mean to tell me the Chicago Tribune's *business* section quoted my stupid joke about Capri pants, but "Puppy Love" is getting no play, not even in dog magazines?" I asked rhetorically, as well as incredulously.

It completely baffled me that I regularly snagged the interest of mainstream publications with frivolous stories about my unruly hair and unfit upper arms, yet a truly touching story about the healing power of pets was routinely ignored by the dog press. After several fruitless attempts to place the story, I just had to let it go. I always felt disappointed that Jif hadn't gotten the public acknowledgement that he deserved, but if Jif felt slighted, he never let it show.

Jif continued to amuse and amaze with his antics and provided comfort during tough transitions, both foreseen—empty nest blues after Torrie's departure for college—and unforeseen, my father's sudden cancer diagnosis and passing. He seemed to instinctively know how to strike the precise balance between being a soft, furry shoulder to cry on and being a dipsy doodle distraction. His balancing skills were never more tested—or more needed—than in the days and weeks after Dick had walked out. Dick had traveled almost constantly during his career, so I was quite accustomed to being home alone. But there is a significant difference between being home alone because a husband is away and being home alone because a husband is gone. The dark of "gone" is infinitely darker, the cold of "gone" is immeasurably colder and the quiet of "gone" is unendurably quieter. It was against these treacherously sharp edges—of dark, cold and quiet— that Jif cushioned me, his sweetness and his silliness, his devotion and his dopiness ensuring that while I would inevitably sustain some wounds, they would not be fatal ones. When non-dog people chided me for allowing Jif to sleep in my bed, I reminded them that of the two "men" who had once shared my bed, the one who walked upright turned out to be the real dog.

In time, Jorge entered the picture, and I anxiously awaited both his reaction to Jif and, more so, Jif's reaction to him because Jif was often fearful of men he didn't know. Jif's timidity around men was due to abuse I suspected he had suffered early in life—probably from the same sub-human piece of garbage who thought throwing him and his brother into a Dumpster and leaving them there to die was an okay thing to do—and each time I saw Jif react fearfully, my heart broke anew. As for Jorge, I had already determined that if I sensed the slightest bit of reluctance on his part to fall madly in love with Jif and declare him the most outrageously spectacular dog in the galaxy, there could be no future for us as a couple. I might be persuaded to spare Jorge's life for such a grievous sin, but he certainly wouldn't be spending any of that life with me.

Their first encounter took place one afternoon at the park where I regularly took Jif to run and swim. Well, wade is more like it because, although clearly a Lab mix, Jif refused to actually swim and would not enter water higher than his chest, no matter how badly he wanted to retrieve the stick floating in water one millimeter deeper. Jorge's car pulled into the parking lot and I swear Jif just *knew* something momentous was happening. He started straining on his leash and doing his excited, high-pitched whimper. He dragged me across the lot to Jorge's car whereupon Jorge put down his window and intoned, *"Hola, hombre!"* At that, Jif went absolutely wild, jumping up on the side of the car and thrusting his head in the open window, practically smacking Jorge in the forehead. I was dumbfounded. Imagine, Jif, bilingual all this time and I'd never had a clue!

It was love at first lick (with Jif doing most of the licking) for this newly minted father and son. They were inseparable from the start and especially enjoyed doing father-and-son activities together at the park, like running around the lake, playing ball in the field, and rolling in horse poop on the riding trails—oh, wait, that last part was only one of them. Jif seemed to come alive in a new way after Jorge came into our lives. Hey, I had been doing the best I could as a single mother raising a son, but a boy needs a father figure. I had already been feeling guilty because shortly after Dick walked out, Jif reverted to squatting instead of lifting his leg. As it turned out, I needn't have worried that he had gender identification issues; apparently, he just got tired of holding his leg aloft for so long. This dog had a serious reservoir inside of him and it took a long time to completely empty. On more than one occasion, I had witnessed him start out by lifting one leg, then change legs midstream, so to speak, and finally just finish the whole thing off in a squat. In all seriousness, though, I felt like I was shortchanging Jif because while I am an excellent cuddler, I am not much of a rough-houser. Jif responded in complete delight to the wrestling, chasing and other forms of horse play that his new daddy engaged in with him. Exhausted after each rousing play session, Jif would then curl up on the bed with me and take full advantage of my snuggling expertise. Obviously, Jorge was what Jif had needed, but I believe Jif was what Jorge had needed as well. It may sound kooky, but Jif helped to ease the aching longing Jorge felt for his sons. At that time, he hadn't seen them for three years, since he'd been forced to seek political asylum in the United States, and he missed them

dreadfully. Jif was proving himself to be a versatile proxy, ably standing in for a runaway husband as well as faraway sons.

As time went by, Jorge and I grew closer to each other (we were
both already adhered to Jif) and married in June of 2006. All of our
adult kids bonded as if they'd been hatched together. Eventually, we
were able to buy a house. Jorge received his citizenship and we were
finally able to visit his family in Colombia. The kids came from their
various continents to spend vacations with us. We even became the
insufferably proud grandparents of an adorable little girl when my
stepson and his wife had their first baby. Little by little, many of the
shattered and scattered pieces of my life had started coalescing into a
new mosaic, with one glaringly empty spot.

The enormous, still-missing piece, the absence of which dampened my spirit every minute of every day, was what I'd always considered my "real" work—reaching out to people through writing and
speaking. I feared that exquisite piece, which had been long deferred
the first time around as it was, was by now irretrievably lost. For many
years during my former marriage, I had worked in public relations,
radio and even on-air in television, but always writing or speaking in
someone else's voice, addressing someone else's concerns, waiting
for the "right" time—and the financial freedom—to be able to focus
on my own voice and my own concerns. Moving seven times in fifteen years to accommodate Dick's career, as well as raising Torrie as
a de facto single parent from birth through age eighteen, had also
continued to push that "right" time further and further into the future.
Finally, though, with Torrie in college and Dick seemingly fully estab-
lished in his career, my turn had come. My first book was published
and led to many great promotional opportunities all over the country,
including TV and radio appearances, speaking engagements and freelance writing offers. I was having the time of my life because I was
doing the thing I enjoy above all else, connecting with people. I am
at heart a performer, no matter what the setting, in front of a classroom, on a talk show set, or in my kitchen. I live to entertain, a goal
that cannot be accomplished in isolation. My book gave me access

to a bigger audience than could be found in my kitchen—even on holidays—and allowed me to make people laugh, reflect and know they were not alone.

The career I had longed for, had dreamed of for so long was in its delicate infancy when the bomb fell on everything in the last days of 2002. At the time, I was only working part-time, teaching English as a Second Language to adults (my other vocational love), and devoting all of my free time to promoting my writing career. Instant and unexpected poverty was a game changer. With every single penny, as well as Dick himself, gone and mountains of debt remaining, part-time work did not cut it. Writing for fun with hopes of eventual profit was not on the survival agenda. I immediately picked up as many extra jobs as I could, at one point working five part-time jobs Monday through Saturday to stave off complete destitution. When, eight months after our divorce was final, Dick announced—from 3,000 miles away—that he was reneging on the alimony agreement, full-blown destitution was on my doorstep. I needed a full-time job immediately. I was incredibly fortunate and within days was referred by a friend for a full-time teaching position in a nearby high school. It broke my heart to leave my ESL adults, and I'd never had any desire to teach kids, but I had no choice if I wanted to avoid living in the street. I was not certified to teach public school at the time, but the school hired me on the spot and allowed me to teach with a provisional certificate until I was able to complete a permanent certification program. Thus began my seven years in exile from writing. I told myself I would continue to write, but there never seemed to be any time. In those seven years of teaching, I was assigned to three different schools, four different grade levels and three different subject areas. Every minute of free time— evenings, weekends and summers—was spent completing the course work for my certification, creating lesson plans, learning constantly changing curricula, and working additional jobs to pay for all the things a teacher's meager salary didn't cover. From the debt Dick left behind to unexpected medical bills to my continually breaking-down car, there was always an urgent need that required my working extra hours. And the truth was, no matter how much I wanted to write, by the end of the day, I was just too worn out to do more than crawl into bed. (And anyone who thinks teaching public school in the 21st century is an "easy" job has no clue! I know I really didn't. Teaching kids nowadays is like what the great Erma Bombeck used to say about housework—that is, if done right, it can kill you.)

One summer Sunday afternoon in 2010—the first summer in many years that I had not had to work—I was sitting in our home office alone except for Jif who was lying on the floor snoring. My fingers poised over the computer keys, my eyes staring at the blank screen, I was trying for all I was worth to begin writing something—*anything*—but could not string together even one prosaic sentence, much less an inspiring one.

"It's gone for good," I said to Jif, referring to my so-called writing career, as I lay down beside him on the floor. I couldn't envision any way that it could come back to me, and that thought weighed my soul down with a heaviness that a husband, a house, or a great haircut could not lift. I felt destined to spend the rest of my life under a veil of sadness and profound disappointment. I was crying into Jif's fur, consumed by feelings of despair, when I heard the ding of a new email. It was from a friend who is very active in animal rescue. She had forwarded me a message about a woman who was writing a book called *The Divinity of Dogs*, a collection of stories about the power dogs have to teach us important spiritual lessons. The publisher was going to make a formal announcement to solicit stories in the near future, but in the meantime, the author was informally polling her "dog people" contacts to see if anyone had a good story to tell. At first, just the idea that someone had a publishing deal—was actually doing what I longed to do again— drove me deeper into the pit of depression. Then, I thought about submitting a story. Of course, submitting a story presupposed I could actually write one, and I'd just spent the entire afternoon proving to myself that I couldn't write a single sentence any more, much less a full story before the short deadline outlined in the message. I was just about to delete the message and continue feeling desperately sorry for myself when Jif stirred and I suddenly thought about my long ago tale, "Puppy Love." I asked Jif what he thought about the idea. He seemed rather indifferent; he'd gotten his hopes up too many times before and was understandably jaded. I decided to submit it and let yet one more person reject it as Jif and I were pretty much immune to rejection by then. I ferreted out the story from the archives of my old life, filled out the submission form and hit "send." Next, I wrote an email to Suzi, the friend who had talked me through my first "date" with Jorge, begging her to reassure me that someday, somehow I would get to do what I loved again. I felt completely hopeless. While I was sitting in front of the monitor, praying for a word of encouragement to appear in my Inbox, the phone rang. I answered it, hoping to hear my friend's voice with a strong dose of hope. It wasn't my friend. Instead, it was Jennifer Skiff, award-winning television journalist and producer, best-selling author of *God Stories*, and...author of the proposed book, *The Divinity of Dogs*. At first, it didn't compute that she was calling me personally, literally fifteen minutes after I had hit the "send" button with "Puppy Love." I listened as she explained that she had just gone into her office to check her email when "Puppy Love" came through. She opened it and started reading it. By the end of the second line, she called for her husband to come and listen to it. When she got to the end, she said, they were both laughing and crying. She said she just felt compelled to pick up the phone and tell me personally how much she loved my story and what a good writer I was.

I was dumbstruck. As in speechless. Certainly not many documented instances of that in history. She asked me all about Jif, about myself and how I came to write the story. I told her how I had been waiting for nearly ten years for "Puppy Love" to be published. She remarked that if it had been published earlier, she couldn't have used it in the book. It may have been a long wait, but, she assured me, Jif's story was going to read by a much bigger audience now than if it had appeared in a newspaper or magazine ten years earlier. Both she and the publisher, no less than Simon and Schuster, expected this book to be an international best-seller as her first book had been. I told her how uncanny the timing was, as I had just been drowning in self-pity, waiting for a word of encouragement from a friend.

"Do you mean you were looking for confirmation that you can write?" she asked.

"Yes," I replied, "I'm just feeling very lost."

"Well then, let me tell you, this call is your confirmation," she said seriously. And then she presented me with the most generous gift I could have received at that moment. "You are a fabulous writer. And I don't tell too many people that." Each word was like a precious pearl dropped into my palm for safekeeping.

She told me the tentative release date for the book was the summer of 2012 and explained all the steps in the process. I hung up the phone and practically collapsed on poor Jif on the floor. I was laughing and crying at the same time, overwhelmed not only by what had just happened, but by the coincidental timing of it. Jif seemed to take the news in stride, rolling over, yawning and dozing off again. Imminent fame didn't faze him. As I said, he was rather jaded by then.

And I believe my spirit started coming the rest of the way back to life that day. It was not an instantaneous resurrection, but from that day on, my desire to write was renewed, and opportunities to do so began to pop up in unexpected places, signposts confirming that I was on the right path. And it all started with Jif. The dog that I hadn't planned on, the dog I hadn't been ready for, the dog I had actually handed back, it was he who had once again come to my rescue and pulled me through a dark time. Oh, how I loved my wild, wonderful and totally whacked out Mr. Jif. As I write these words today, the release date for *The Divinity of Dogs* is less than two months away. In less than two months people (and dogs) the world over will be able to read about the amazing Mr. Jif, as well as feast their eyes upon his handsome visage. How I have looked forward to the arrival of this day. And every time I have imagined this day in my mind, Mr. Jif was at my side, possibly autographing copies of the book for all his dog friends. But that scene is not to be because Mr. Jif, my sweet, silly savior, is no longer here.

One September afternoon last year Jorge and I took Jif to the vet because he had been limping off and on for a week or so. He was still recovering from the $1,500 worth of surgery he'd had in April to repair a ruptured ACL caused by a surprise hit from a rambunctious Australian shepherd. Don't tell me, I thought, now his other back leg needs surgery. Torrie's wedding was in two weeks and resources were stretched rather tightly.

"I think he's just mad that we're spending more money on his sister than on him and he wants to even the score," I jokingly told Rick, our veterinarian.

"Well, let's just check this boy out," Rick said as he bent down to examine Jif. As Rick's face passed Jif's, Jif's tongue wasted no time sneaking in a few licks. He was such a kissy boy. Jorge and I were chatting away, anticipating a diagnosis that might bruise our wallets, but certainly not one that would crush our hearts.

"Okay, let me have it, how much is it going to cost to fix this leg?" I asked jokingly.

Rick looked at both us for a moment and then stated in a quiet tone that he needed to have an X-ray to confirm his suspicions.

"But, you need to know his symptoms present very much like bone cancer," Rick said soberly.

All the air went out of my lungs and my knees buckled under me. Jorge steadied me with his arms and our tear-filled eyes met. Cancer? What was he talking about? It wasn't possible. Jif was fine. He just hurt his leg; that's all. My God, who ever said anything about cancer? That was never the plan!

"No, that's not possible. He's not even sick," I said definitively, hoping to talk Rick out of his diagnosis.

"Yes, he is eating and running all the time," said Jorge, bolstering my argument.

"Let's just get the X-ray and go from there," Rick said gently and led Jif out of the exam room. Jif went readily, tail a-wagging, probably hoping to get a cookie.

Jorge and I stood trembling, both breathing out the word "no" over and over again as we waited for Rick and Jif to come back. "Oh, please, no," I prayed in my heart. "Please don't take this boy from me now. Not my sweet boy, please, no."

The X-ray confirmed what we already knew, but didn't want to accept. While Rick outlined the likely course of events, Jif, bored with the whole deal, paced around the exam room, licked hands, scratched at the door, and jumped up against the counter, angling for one of the Milk Bones Rick kept in a plastic container. Normally, I would have scolded him for showing such bad manners, but right then I wanted to dump the whole container on the floor for him; right then I would have built him a Milk Bone factory from scratch if that's what he had wanted, if he would have just promised not to leave us.

We had three more months with our boy, and I divided my time between hugging him to squeeze love in and hugging him to wring love out, to store away for the lonely days ahead. Throughout the final days of his journey, Jif remained, amazingly, very much himself. We were, thankfully, able to keep him comfortable with medication, and he continued his daily routine of eating, playing and barking serious warnings to the orange cat that hunted among the junipers in our back yard. And, ironically, he never limped again. Even as the wretchedly invasive tumor grew larger, claiming more and more of his leg, Jif never limped. He continued to trot around the house and yard, just as he always had.

And yet, he was not exactly as he had always been; he seemed to have developed an awareness, a kind of knowing, that our time together was limited because he stayed very close to both of us all the time. We used to call him Mr. Independent because he would often pick up and leave us alone in the living room while he went off to nap somewhere else. We joked that that he liked to "sleep around" because he would roam from room to room, and we were never quite sure where we would find him snoozing—in a corner of the guest room, on the treadmill in the office or under the vanity in the bathroom. But those last three months, he never once went off alone when we were home with him. He stayed by our sides and began resting his head in our laps when we sat down, as if for reassurance that we would be with him every step of the way, as he had been for us. Even asleep he seemed to need us close. Instead of sleeping on his bed in the corner of our bedroom, he lay on the floor right beside our bed, alternating between my side and Jorge's side throughout the night.

In the end, the greedy tumor consumed the bone, and the weakened leg just gave way. Even then, Jif's reaction was so subdued we weren't sure what had happened. Late one evening we were with him in the back yard when he simply stood up, let out one single yelp and drew his leg up tightly against his body. We ran to him and, apart from holding his leg off the ground, he seemed perfectly normal. We stroked and soothed him, and then Jorge scooped him up and carried him into the house.

Jorge took him back to the vet the next day alone because I had to teach until 9:00 p.m. Rick confirmed that the bone had indeed broken, and that it was time. Because it was the week before Christmas, my students were in the middle of final exams, and I could not miss even one class. Rick told Jorge that if we could keep Jif quiet and comfortable at home, we could wait two days until my next evening off to bring him back together.

I will never be able to express my gratitude for the gift of that extra time. We moved Jif's food and water into our bedroom and he lived in there for the next two days. He stood up to eat, drink and shift his position now and then, but otherwise, he was content to doze off and on and lick our faces when we lay beside him on the floor. Several times a day, Jorge carried him outside and then back to the bedroom. The first time I witnessed this unbearably poignant scene, I broke down in sobs. I couldn't help thinking that Jorge looked like a painting of The Good Shepherd, carrying the lost sheep back to the fold. I never loved Jorge more than at that moment. And Jif, who had always protested being carried, was at ease, resting securely in his father's arms. I never loved Jif more than at that moment either. Our boy Jif had always been equal parts sweet and sassy, but, in those final days, it seemed that the sassy completely dissolved into the sweet. In the end, there was nothing but pure, distilled, heartbreaking sweetness remaining. Sweetness concentrate. And then, at that saturation point, it was time to let him go. We made the final trip to the veterinarian's office as three, and returned home as two—broken-hearted, but also enormously grateful for having had this insanely wonderful dog in our lives for so long.

And so, in a few weeks, when I finally get to read "Puppy Love" in its official, published form, I will wince a bit that my boy isn't here to share the moment. But I will try to believe that he felt he had done all he had come here to do. He had eased my grief over losing Ruckus, comforted me through a horrific divorce, helped me cement my new family together and, finally, accomplished what I had never imagined possible, revived my writing career. I guess he felt it was okay for him to move on. So, good-bye, my dear, sweet Mr. Jif. Thank you for twelve amazing years, for being there through laughter and tears. You were so loved, and, oh, how very much you are missed.

11

Not Always Happily Ever Laughter

"I CAN REMEMBER the day, the moment, actually, that it felt like something inside of me just broke. I fell into a very dark place, crying endlessly, often for no obvious reason," says the woman being interviewed on TV. I relate so well to what she is saying, understand those exact feelings…because that woman is, in fact, me. I am watching a videotape of myself doing a talk show interview about my experience with depression. It may seem a bit incongruous to talk about depression in a book advocating humor as a survival tool, but I would not be honest if I didn't admit that there have been times in my life when the laughter stopped and I felt helpless to restart it on my own.

First, Some History

As a teenager, I thought I knew what depression was and actually embraced it, thinking it lent an air of tortured sophistication to my bad confessional poetry. As I came to appreciate some years later, however, adolescent angst born largely of break-outs and break-ups is merely melodrama, not clinical depression. I first fell into the abyss of real depression in 1999 when I was still married to Dick. The fall seemed to have happened in an instant, but eventually I was able to recognize that the path leading to the edge had been a long one. I have since learned that it is not unusual for people to function perfectly through a protracted crisis and then crash into depression afterward. Throughout the summer of 1998, I was crisscrossing the country nearly nonstop, promoting my first book, which had just been released. I would often cover two or three different cities, or even states, in one day. It was a tiring schedule, but altogether exciting and rewarding. The pleasure of that experience, however, was seriously blunted by the substantial stress of executing a move from Atlanta to Chicago for Dick's job transfer during that same time. (See Chapter 9, "Home Sweet Homicide," for details.)

When we finally arrived in Chicago the last week of August 1998, the stress did not abate. With Dick traveling constantly, I was left to supervise a slew of painters, carpenters, carpet installers and other craftsmen, as they worked to undo the damage that the previous owner had inflicted on our house. I was living in a four-floor labyrinth of unpacked boxes, power tools and ladders, and coughing up drywall dust in my sleep. Endless lengths of industrial-strength extension cords snaked in and around every square inch of living space, making going to the bathroom in the middle of the night more dangerous than crossing a minefield. It was a bit stressful. At the same time, I was trying to keep my book publicity on a roll in a new city, uncover freelance writing opportunities, smooth Torrie's transition to a new high school and adjust to the horrifying image that confronted me in the mirror every day thanks to a new hair stylist dyeing the gray roots of my dark brown hair jet black by mistake.

In the midst of all the turmoil, came many exciting developments as well. I found a fantastic publicist who routinely secured excellent promotional opportunities for my book, including regular TV appearances, newspaper and magazine coverage. She also helped me land a great writing position with a local magazine, so when I wasn't being interviewed myself, I was out interviewing some of the most interesting and exciting people in the city. My dream life was materializing before my eyes. Still, I felt like someone had dumped my life into a blender set on high, as everything was whirling around me so fast. I couldn't wait until Christmas when I estimated many of the wrinkles of our move would be smoothed out, allowing me to fully enjoy our new life in Chicago. By Christmas, I figured the work on the house would be complete, Dick would be home for more than a day at a time and surely, I hoped, Torrie would be adjusted to her new school. I was holding fast to that thought, even through the pop-up storm that thoroughly drenched my dining room furniture, which had been temporarily relocated to the patio while workers sanded the floors; even through concerned calls from my parents' physicians about some necessary surgery for both of them; even through growing worry about my sister's deteriorating health; and even through the daily humiliation of walking around with the hair of Elvira, Mistress of the Dark. "C'mon, Christmas," I repeated to myself every time I felt I was going to lose it. And then, the bottom fell out of my Christmas hope. On December 17, Ruckus, my much beloved English Springer Spaniel, who had been ailing for several months, reached a crisis point and had to be laid to rest. I had never had to make that decision for a pet before and the weight of it, along with the tremendous sense of loss, was very difficult for me. My spirits were definitely dampened during Christmas. On the heels of this great sadness came a stunning announcement on January 5th. Dick came home from work and told me he had been fired, effective immediately, from his job of eleven years—a mere four months after his company had relocated our entire lives to Chicago for his new position. Reeling violently from this unexpected development, I then got a message from my gynecologist on January 7th, informing me that suspicious new findings on my mammogram required follow-up tests and needle biopsies. Furthermore, she said, with so many anomalous findings, the radiologist had suggested that I consider having my breasts mapped. Really, that's what she said, mapped. This was before the days of GPS, so I assumed they planned to use a sextant and a compass. The specter of breast mapping may have been the breaking point for me.

Dick tackled the job search and I began scheduling my doctors' appointments. He actually landed a new position back in Atlanta before I knew definitively the verdict on my breasts. After consults with two radiologists and a surgeon, an hour-long "mapping session" and a needle-guided biopsy attempt that was curtailed when the radiologist almost punctured my lung, it was decided that watchful waiting was a better course. I would need to have ultrasound examinations of my breasts every three months for a year before the "suspicious findings" were declared benign cysts—"debris-filled," but benign all the same. (Debris-filled, really? Like, with lint? Old gum wrappers, Cheez-it crumbs, what?)

The whammies of December and January hit me hard. By February, I didn't recognize myself. I was crying several times every day at the slightest provocation or with no provocation at all. I had a constant headache that translated into my being unable think clearly or make even the simplest decision. One day I actually ran out of the grocery store, shaking with panic, because I had picked up a package of hot dogs, but couldn't remember what went with them—uh, that would be buns. I became so agitated and confused at my inability to make that connection that I threw down the hot dogs, ran out to my car and drove home without buying anything. It was as if information would not process. I was plagued by insomnia and early morning waking, exacerbating my headaches and foggy thinking. I had also adopted a kind of uniform when I was at home because even trying to decide what clothes to put on seemed overwhelming to me. For most of the winter of 1999, my "look" consisted of blue leggings, blue shirt, blue socks and blue shoes. I would put the clothes in the laundry at night and wear them again the next day. Day by day, my affect became flatter and flatter, I spoke less and less and the weight of hopelessness and despair became heavier and heavier. I wanted only to sit on the couch alone and stare into space—which I could do for hours on end. This is not a good thing for someone promoting a humor book.

Ironically, in the end, my struggle with depression led to great opportunities to promote my book. When my blue leggings started looking a little threadbare, I finally faced the fact that I needed help. I called an old friend, a noted psychiatrist, who immediately—and very graciously—got me hooked up with an excellent psychiatrist in Chicago and later in Atlanta. Despite my initially strong resistance

to taking antidepressants, I finally agreed to give the prescribed reg-
imen a try. Wow! What an amazing difference serotonin makes! I
turned out to be among the fortunate who have a very positive and,
in my case, nearly immediate, response to antidepressant therapy.
Within weeks I was feeling and acting like my old self again—laughing, dancing and expanding my wardrobe beyond blue leggings. By
then Dick had moved back to Atlanta to begin his new job. I stayed
behind in Chicago for a few months to allow Torrie to finish up the
quarter at school—which by then she absolutely loved and did not
want to leave, of course—as well as wrap up the sale of the house and
coordinate the move back to Atlanta, the reverse of the very move we
had made less than a year before. I know if I had not sought help for
the depression, I would have been unable to handle those duties. The
only painful aspect of the move that antidepressants or talk therapy
could not ameliorate was my genuine disappointment at having to
leave a city, a lifestyle and work that I had fallen in love with. It was
the life I had waited so long to live and it hurt immeasurably to have
to let it go. But, I had no choice, so I put on my big girl panties, and
headed back from whence I had just come. One day not long after
we had moved back to Atlanta and after I was well into depression recovery, I happened to be in my psychiatrist's office when he received
a media request to discuss research he was doing. The TV news producer wanted to interview a patient if possible. My doctor put the
producer on hold and asked me if I would be comfortable talking on
camera about my response to treatment. Comfortable talking, me?
Hell, I'd not only talk, I'd script, film and edit the damn thing, if they
wanted! In short order, I grabbed the phone out of his hand, suggested the "depressed humor writer" angle to the producer—which
she loved—and ended up doing about ten or so interviews for local
stations and cable networks around the country. For a few months
there I think every media outlet doing a story on mental health had
me on speed dial (possibly under dial-a-nut)!

As reluctant as I had been to leave my life in Chicago, I had to
admit that the move back to Atlanta had worked out very well. My

dream life was reconfiguring and materializing again. I had begun work on my second book, was landing a number of freelance writing opportunities and had begun teaching English as a Second Language classes part-time, which became a true passion for me. I had developed such a strong relationship with the media in Chicago that I even continued to be invited back there to speak on various topics, including depression. I was slowly weaned off the antidepressants and continued to feel more than well; I was quite excited about the direction my life was taking and was anticipating even bigger and better things to come—ignorance being so very blissful and all.

Back to the Future

Fast forward to 2010, more than seven years after the initial bomb drop that blasted apart the infrastructure of my life and set off the chain reaction of unending chaos and destruction that I've shared in the preceding chapters, as well as much more that I haven't shared. By that point in time, I was also feeling the full effects of the hormonal hell of menopause. Mine was definitely *not* the pause that refreshes, unless you consider blinding migraines, constant nausea, nightly heart palpitations, painfully inflamed joints, crippling Plantar fasciitis and chronic insomnia refreshing. And don't forget gaining thirty unexplained pounds, my hair falling out in chunks and developing food sensitivities that resulted in my previously porcelain complexion erupting more violently than Mt. St. Helens. I carried on—more like lumbered on, lugging so much excess physical and psychic baggage—day after day for seven years without ever really falling apart, not because I am so strong and capable, but because I honestly did not have time to collapse. It seemed like plugging up one leak only to have three more spring up in its place was business as usual most days. Here's a very partial list of the exciting and budget-busting, hence even more stress-inducing, events that filled my "free" time— you know, the seven minutes when I wasn't working my various part-time jobs before and after my regular eight-hour workday to try to dig my way out of Dick's legacy of mountainous debt: my car's frequent and costly breakdowns; $1,200 to evict squatter squirrels from my attic and repair the damage they caused; a clogged sewer line which filled the first floor of my apartment with raw waste two inches deep; ongoing breast tests as well as tests for uterine cancer, all of which my new insurance deemed pre-existing conditions and would not pay for; Jif's extensive and expensive testing and treatment for thyroid problems; my broken molar and the resulting $5,000 root canal and crown; plus these just-for-fun freebies—Jorge's pneumonia, appendicitis, kidney stone and shingles.

Oh, I flirted with depression at the odd moments when I actually had a chance to breathe and let myself fully feel, but I never really went over the edge. There was no room in my schedule. Friends and colleagues often commented on how well I was functioning through the unfolding crises of my life, handling all the stress and still smiling every day. (Many also jokingly expressed their disbelief that I hadn't considered "taking out a contract" on Dick. I am Italian and Jorge is Colombian, but, damn, we didn't know a single hit man between the two of us. Go figure.)

Early in 2010 my convincing game face began cracking around the edges. In the space of 26 months, I had lost three close friends to cancer, which shattered not only a good portion of my game face, but of my heart as well. Seeing the lives of those three courageous women cut so short only intensified the urgency I already felt to regain the passion and joy that had once infused my life, particularly my work life. After seven years of operating in crisis mode and working two and three jobs at a time just to keep my head above water, I was completely burned out. I could almost hear the grains of sand streaming through my hourglass and I knew that I desperately needed to make some changes, but I didn't know how or where to start. As much as I enjoyed teaching, and as grateful as I was for the extra jobs that had allowed me to keep food on my table, it had never been my intention to abandon my nascent writing and speaking career. That was the path of my dreams, the one I believed was my true calling and which gave me an intense pleasure and satisfaction that I found nowhere else. Unfortunately, it had become collateral damage in my ongoing struggle for survival. There had been neither time nor inspiration for taking even baby steps along that path for seven years, and I longed for it so deeply that I sometimes felt like I couldn't breathe. The fear that I would never find my way back to it was so debilitating that I could not function if I allowed myself to feel it, so I tried to repress it as best I could. I patched up my game face and just soldiered on, telling myself it would happen "someday."

Repression is never very effective as a long-term plan, of course, and by mid-2010, the panicked despair that I daily tried so hard to push down was pushing back with tremendous force. When I locked the door on my 6th-grade "portable classroom" at the end of that school year, it was as if I had flipped a switch inside of myself as well. That final door click that typically triggers a sigh of relief in teachers everywhere triggered a deep sigh of anguish in me. With the pressure of multiple deadlines lifted, all of the feelings I had been repressing came bubbling up to the surface. I barely made it to my car before I broke down in huge, gulping sobs. I did not want to lose control in front of everyone, so I quickly drove off. Less than a mile from the school, I was so overtaken by emotion that I had to pull into an empty church parking lot. That's when the dam truly broke. I shuddered as wails of grief—anguished, tortured cries that came from a very primal and wounded place—poured out of me. I had spent the previous seven years trying desperately to stay afloat in a tsunami of turmoil, had tried, despite all the bad breaks and wrong turns, to hold onto a small corner of my dream, hoping somehow to preserve it for the time when I entered calmer waters, for "someday." Yet it seemed that all my struggle and determination had come to naught. I still hadn't reached those hoped-for calmer waters; my dream was nowhere in sight. In seven years' time I had accomplished nothing but growing seven years older. Seven years of my life wasted, merely treading water, going nowhere. I was old—and now fat, balding and limping to boot—and teaching in a trailer. I was a million miles away from my dream. "Someday" didn't exist.

After several minutes, I caught my breath, opened my eyes and looked around, trying to get my bearings. My car may have been in the middle of a parking lot, but I recognized where my spirit really was—in the abyss. I was no longer dancing around it or teetering on the brink, I was all the way down at the bottom of it. And I really couldn't believe there was any way out for me this time.

After sitting in an armchair the entire first week of summer vacation, alternately crying and staring for most of the day, I gave in and called a psychiatrist. I had absolutely no faith whatsoever that I would ever feel better this time. This time was different, I told myself. This time was not a temporary bad bump in the road; I needed a whole new life and I didn't know of any therapist or antidepressants that could give me that. This kind of thinking, however, that there is no hope, is one of the cruelest lies of depression. A depressed mind deceives you into believing that you will never feel better, that there are no answers for you and that it is utterly pointless to seek treatment. It is true, of course, that no medication or therapist can "give you a whole new life," but effective treatment helps heal your mind enough to entertain possibilities and allows you to envision a path you could not see through the cloud of depression.

After two months of couch time—wherein my therapist assured me I was the most entertaining a client he'd ever had, thereby convincing me I hadn't lost my sense of humor—and a bit of pharmaceutical support, the storm clouds finally began to part. And no, I didn't get a whole new life, but I did rebuild my strength and resolve, which enabled me to embrace anew a belief I have always espoused but have often lost hold of—that time is not retrievable, but it is redeemable. It is true—and often more than a little tragic—that we cannot go back and recover time that has been "lost" to us, but we can make that time count by wringing every last bit of meaning out of it and using those lessons to move toward a better future. I began doing that during the summer of 2010, making plans for my future, and taking small, but intentional steps on a road that I hoped would finally lead me in the right direction. Not working that summer gave me time to reintroduce into my life all the things that had been sacrificed in service to my financial survival the past several years. Simple, but important, things, things that had always fed my soul, such as spending time with friends, taking long walks, writing in my journal.

And, amazingly, out of the blue I began receiving little confirmations—itty bitty ones, but more than I'd seen in years—that I was indeed heading in the right direction. It was in the middle of the summer of 2010 that I received the phone call from Jennifer Skiff regarding my story about Jif which truly was the spark that rekindled my writing career. Then near the end of that summer, I got another small, but rather dramatic, confirmation when I was approached by a total stranger at an educational conference. He had just seen me participate in an impromptu marketing presentation on stage that had gone over very well with the audience.

He sought me out between sessions and said, "Is there a reason you are not a fulltime professional speaker or performer?" I had no idea who he was and had no time to respond to his question before the crowd separated us.

He called back to me over the heads of the crowd, "You should be doing this professionally."

Who was that masked man, I thought to myself. I tried to follow his trail through the crowd with my eyes, but lost sight of him when several of my coworkers pulled me by the elbow to go to lunch. When we returned to the conference for the afternoon session, I couldn't get what the mystery man had said to me off my mind, and I was disappointed that I hadn't had the chance to find out who he was—some nut or someone who knew what he was talking about.

"Oh, well, I guess I'll never know," I said under my breath, as I sat through the introduction for the keynote speaker. Imagine my surprise then when the speaker made his way to the stage and I saw that it was none other than my mystery man! I now know him as Kent Julian, a very successful speaker, published author and life coach, and feel confident in saying he is both someone who knows what he's talking about *and* "some nut." I ended up becoming part of a public speaker's training program that Kent headed up, and the connections I made through that group and through Jennifer's book, *The Divinity of Dogs*, have proved invaluable in propelling me further along the path toward my dream. With the publication of this book and the other writing and speaking opportunities that have come my way recently, I feel more confident than ever that this time I really can make my dream path a reality.

Not a single one of my "lost" years can ever be retrieved, but I am placing my hope in their eventual redemption. I urge you to do the same and to reach out for whatever help you need to build—or rebuild!—the life you deserve, the life we all deserve, the life of "happily ever laughter."

12

Tell Two Jokes and Call
Me in the Morning

"MY, MY, MY...MY dear," said Dr. Traylor, the endocrinologist, shaking his head both in sympathy and disbelief. "You have certainly endured a long series of calamities. It sounds like a book."

"Well, I intend it to be one," I replied. "And it had better be a best-seller. I deserve something for my extensive time and trouble. Something in addition to the thinning hair, thickening waistline and adult acne that I've acquired so far!" I laughed.

"And that's why you are here sitting in front of me today," he commented.

"Yes, that, plus the swollen joints, insomnia and gastric distress," I continued. "I'm the complete package, baby. Value added."

"No, that's not what I meant," he explained. "I meant the fact that you still have a sense of humor. That is why you are sitting in front of me after navigating some very rough waters. That's why you are here and not in a psychiatric hospital or worse, in the ground."

"Well, trust me, some days I'm not all that humorous," I assured him. "Some days the total in that loss column seems a very hard deficit to overcome. Some days the ground looks pretty good to me."

"I understand and I'm not in any way minimizing what you've been through," Dr. Traylor continued. "But you need to realize that your ability to use humor, and I'm guessing even dark humor, has been critical to your survival. Many people lack a good coping mechanism and loss defeats them. It can be faith or hope or gratitude, but people need something to hold onto through tough times. And humor, with its ability to discharge both emotional and physical stress, is a very important part of being resilient, of coming back after a crisis. So, whether you knew it or not, whether it was intentional or not, you gave yourself a great advantage in a very bad situation."

"Well, thanks, I guess, but I should tell you that I also mainlined diet Coke," I said.

"Well, if that's the worst substance you abused, be grateful," he laughed. "Now, with what you've been through, it's going to be a challenge for me to determine which troublesome symptoms are menopausal and which are the result of massive and protracted stress. But, I am going to figure it out and get you feeling better."

With that, he took off to go order some tests for me. By time I reached Dr. Traylor's office that day, I had been through three gynecologists, one primary care doctor and two endocrinologists during the previous four years, trying to get some help for a slew of physical ailments that had started seemingly within minutes of my last period stopping. It had to have been the fastest onset of menopause on record. Why did I always seem to set the wrong kinds of records? So far, each trip to the doctor had been a dead end for my myriad symptoms, but I felt hopeful about this one. Maybe it was because he had taken the time to listen to me and that he'd been interested enough in me as a whole person to see my symptoms within the context of my life. And most importantly, he acknowledged that I had experienced some monumentally hard and unfair things and had done a pretty damn good job handling them.

Something just that simple, having someone acknowledge your struggle, can help you weather a terrible storm. For me, it wasn't that I wanted to wallow in self-pity or play the martyr, but I did need to know that I wasn't crazy for feeling overwhelmed by the sharp curve balls life had thrown me. Acknowledgement affirmed to me that I had legitimate cause to feel overwhelmed, and, interestingly enough, gave me the strength to persevere.

Our culture is so impatient and uncomfortable with any problem that does not neatly resolve itself in one episode of Dr. Phil. We don't like to be confronted with suffering. We quickly look away from other people's honestly displayed pain because it might make us look at our own or it might compel us to lend a hand, and often we don't want to be troubled with either. The "get over it, move on" response that our society seems so enamored of has become an easy out for people who want to avoid either examining their own pain and loss or offering support to others who are seeking authentic healing from loss. The insensitive and uninformed minimizing that a poorly placed "get over it" represents is extremely hurtful to someone in a genuine crisis.

I love the joke about the guy who was devastated when, without warning, his wife left him. His friend said, "Oh, man, you just need to get over it." The guy responded, "But she just walked out on me this morning." To which the friend replied, "And yet, here we are four hours later still talking about it."

I swear Dick had only been gone three weeks—third week of January—when he told me and others that I just needed to move on and stop living in the past. He comes by his denial and detachment honestly. Shortly after he walked out on Torrie and me, his mother wrote me a letter telling me, and I quote, "it's time to just put your marriage away in your memory box." Yes, 23 years of my life and the ticket stub from my first Fleetwood Mac concert, it's pretty much the same. Tuck it away in the memory box, close the lid, all done, good as new. Hardly.

My intention is not to bash my ex-husband or his family—well, not any more than absolutely necessary, ha, ha—it's to point out how drastically out of touch many folks are and how destructive that level of detachment is. There is a grand difference between getting over something and glossing over something. I think most people prefer the superficial glossing over option that masquerades as optimism or a positive attitude, but is actually denial and avoidance. Yes, getting over something is the ultimate goal, but a goal is what is reached *after* a process has taken place. There is no shortcut for achieving the goals of true resolution and acceptance. You cannot get there without going through a process of thoughtful reflection, of genuine grieving. But reflecting and grieving are messy and time-consuming, so we tell people to get over it because we don't want to be bothered getting down in the dirt with them. Not to mention, telling someone whom you have deeply wronged to get over it is a very convenient way to avoid taking any responsibility for your actions. It's the ultimate get-out-of-jail-free card. I can hear the infomercial now: *"Committed any reprehensible, unconscionable acts? Atrocious abuses of trust? Don't waste time with acknowledgements or apologies! Forget restitution! Now, there's the 'Get Over It,' the quick and easy way to shift blame, let yourself off the hook and pretend like nothing ever happened! Supplies unlimited, so toss a few today!"*

How very cavalier…and cowardly.

All of those thoughts flooded my brain as I sat alone that day, waiting for Dr. Traylor to return, but I couldn't deny the small spark of hope I felt inside as well. Ironically, nothing in my physical being had miraculously changed since I had walked in the door an hour before. I still had painfully inflamed joints and tendons, bags under my eyes from not sleeping for weeks, thirty pounds of unexplained weight gain, hair the texture of straw, heart palpitations and a migraine; yet, I felt better than I had in years—because I felt validated and understood, and that is the beginning of all authentic healing.

"Okay, I have you all set up for next Wednesday," said Dr. Traylor as he breezed back into the office. He carefully explained how this battery of tests would help him determine the best way to bring back "the old me."

"Any chance of a new and improved version instead?" I suggested. "Like, Lee 2.0, is that too much to ask from modern science?"

Dr. Traylor laughed. "No need to update a classic. For right now, just go home and keep that sense of humor in place."

"You mean I should tell two jokes and call you in the morning?" I asked.

"Yes," he replied, smiling. "I told you, laughter really *is* the best medicine."

13

Gratitude and the Power of Enough

AS I WRITE these words now in 2013, my life is on more secure footing than in the past several years, but that footing still gives way around the edges. My life may never completely return to the way it was "before." I don't suppose there is ever a good time to lose everything, but I can attest to the fact that age 45 is definitely not the optimum time. Not only do you have a lot more to lose at 45 than 25, but you have much less time to recover the resources you will need to support yourself through old age. Short of hitting the lottery, it is all but impossible to make up for twenty years of lost savings and investments. And you have more obligations to meet at 45 than you did at 25. A cliché is a cliché because it resonates universally, and I certainly found out the truth of the cliché "If you think money isn't important, try living without it." Living day in and day out under intense financial pressure exacts a costly toll on all aspects of your health. There were days in the past ten years when I was hanging on by such a slim thread that if I had dropped a quarter in a parking lot and it had rolled under a car, I would have crawled through grease and grime on my belly to retrieve it with my teeth because being short 25 cents meant the difference between being able to pay my rent and not!

At the same time, there is so much cause for gratitude. Dr. Traylor really did figure out how to help me and I am now pain-free, with hair and weight back to normal, or as normal as can be expected for a 55-year-old woman who could really do with one of those Lifestyle Lifts—although given the extensive square footage of all that is falling on me, I'm thinking a "lift" won't do it. Maybe a Lifestyle Hoist.

Of course, I am grateful beyond measure for all the usual suspects: my sweet Jorgito, who fearlessly took on the unfolding catastrophe of my life and whose love and support for me have never wavered. He has been my rock; my beautiful daughter Torrie, whom I have had the pleasure of seeing graduate from college and embark on a very successful career and who gave me the distinct honor of walking her down the aisle to meet her handsome and brilliant groom David; my amazingly talented and impossibly attractive step-family, comprised of dashing sons Jorge Andres and Eduardo, lovely daughters-in-law, Lily and Nathalia, and one little Miss Gabriela, adorable granddaughter. Plus, a delightful contingent of in-laws and even a few wonderful outlaws. I am so grateful for the good they have brought to my life.

But, I must also share my immense gratitude for having learned "the power of enough." I didn't even know there was such a thing, much less that I had learned it, until someone pointed it out and named it for me. I was batting around some ideas with my speaker's group and was asking the other members for feedback on a presentation I was preparing about using humor to tolerate the absurdities of life. I am great with spinning an entertaining yarn and pointing out the opportunities for sanity-saving laughs in even the most bizarre situations, but I felt like I was missing the big lesson that tied it all together.

"I can talk about all the things that have happened to me, and address the humor in those discrete instances, which is important," I said, "but what's the big takeaway lesson?"

"Well, tell me right now, in five seconds—what did you learn from everything that happened," commanded Dan.

"Uh, don't marry my ex-husband again? Don't let your dog run in a cow pasture? Geez, Dan, I don't know. Oh, my gosh, I haven't learned anything big at all! I am a moron!"

We all laughed, but I was serious, too. What if there really was no overall meaning to everything I had gone through? What if it was just a series of incredibly crappy, but random experiences, adding up to nothing? How could that be of any value to others?

"Think of your worst day, why didn't you give up?" Dan asked with urgency.

"I thought things might get better," I answered uncertainly, with a shrug of my shoulders.

"Why would you think that? Things were terrible. You thought the entire universe, including God, hated you. Why didn't you give up?" he continued to batter away at me.

"I *hoped* things would get better," I re-phrased.

"Hope? Where did you find hope? Wasn't everything terrible?" Dan was relentless.

"Yes, but..."

"But what? Was everything terrible or not?"

"Well, many, many things were very, very terrible, but not everything," I said, sounding like I was trying to convince him now, instead of myself, as had been true all those times in the past ten years. I continued with conviction. "Lots of times, 99% of the things were terrible, but I'd somehow find the 1% that wasn't. And that little scrap was enough to get me through."

"Aha," said Dan. "So you did learn something, an invaluable lesson. You learned to appreciate the power of enough."

I had never thought of it that way, but he was right. None of my problems in the past ten years had been magically solved with a wave of the hand. There had been no dramatic rescue scenes, no *deus ex machina* appearing at the last minute to set things completely aright, no matter how much I had yearned for that. But, every time I felt I was really and truly at the end of my rope, even as my head ranted about the futility of holding on for one more day, my heart would seek out and latch onto a small sign of hope. And that small sign had been enough for that moment. Each time I had really needed it, a little piece of enough came to me. I'd be praying with absolute desperation and look up to see skywriting—I am not kidding, this happened—that said, "God loves you." (And my first blasphemous thought was, nice sentiment, God, but could you say it with cash?) Another time, I was sitting in my parked car, crying and feeling as if I would never, ever recover my life, when I looked up just in time to see the writing on the side of a passing truck that read, "Full circle restoration is coming to you." One time I contributed the last five dollars in my wallet—every cent I had to get me through two weeks until the next payday—to a breast cancer fundraiser at work and went home to find a completely unexpected gift from a friend in the mail, a check for five hundred dollars, one hundred times the amount I had donated. Oh, and by the way, the friend was a breast cancer patient at the time. Call them weird coincidences, but I now call them "enough."

Often, an "enough" answer to our heartfelt prayer can touch us more profoundly and teach us more enduring lessons than the "perfect" answer can. One of the most powerful demonstrations of "enough" I have experienced occurred a few years back while un-packing Christmas decorations. I love Christmas and I regress to the emotional maturity of a six year old when it comes time to decorate each year. I am giddy with excitement and also stubbornly bent on arranging every last sprig of holly "perfectly." One of the most painful aspects of losing my house and having to live in the contact lens case for three years was not having a spare inch of space to decorate for Christmas beyond hanging a red dish towel on a kitchen hook. Every time I walked past Christmas displays in stores during those years, I felt a sharp stabbing in my heart. I prayed that someday I would be able to celebrate Christmas with all the trimmings in a house of my own again. The first year that Jorge and I were able to do just that, I, just like all the reindeer, shouted out with glee as I unpacked all of my Christmas treasures that had been stowed away for so long. I squealed with delight as I opened each box and greeted every angel and snowman like long lost friends, which in many ways they were. Until I opened the last box. In that box was my much beloved set of Christmas putz houses (some call them glitter houses) that I'd bought several years before. The little painted cardboard houses were not antique ones or even expensive. I'd bought them at Target, for heaven's sake, but they meant a great deal to me because they reminded me of the old ones my family had had when I was a child, none of which had survived three children playing with them. My tears of delight at seeing them again quickly turned to tears of despair as, unwrapping them, I found they had become misshapen from being packed away so long. Well, talk about regressing to the maturity level of a six year old—my reaction was a bit out of proportion to the "tragedy." I believe I handled my father's death with more composure. I wailed and moaned, stomped my feet and pounded my fists. I would have thrown myself on the floor in a full-out kicking and screaming tantrum, but I have a bad back and wasn't sure I could get back up! At that moment I felt as if those smashed and dented putz houses were a message to me, cruelly mocking all of my efforts to reclaim important pieces of my life. More than being a metaphor for all that had been destroyed, they seemed to be telling me that any efforts I'd made or would make in the future would be futile, that too much damage had been done for me to ever recover.

Jorge calmly suggested that I go online and search for replacements, which I finally did after loud protestations and dramatic proclamations that it would be useless because didn't he know nothing would ever work out right for me, ever again! With me and my ranting somewhat contained in another room, he was free to do what he has done from the start—be my more-than-enough answer to prayer. Engineer that he is, he fashioned a kind of "house steamer" by placing a grease screen atop a boiling pot of water. He set each house on the grease screen just long enough to make the cardboard pliable, and then he ever so gently coaxed each house back into its original shape.

After each house had cooled and "gelled," he called me to come see what he had done. My jaw dropped in confusion when I saw the houses. They looked almost as good as new. He explained what he had done, and I couldn't even thank him because my inner six year old was blubbering too violently to speak. I couldn't believe the wonderful gift he had just given me. Again. It's true the houses weren't exactly perfect anymore. The church suffers from a permanent, but slight, curvature of the steeple and a few fence posts will forever lean a bit out of kilter, but they are beyond perfect in my eyes; indeed, they are "enough."

When I finished relaying these instances to my speaker's group, everyone was quiet for a moment. Then Dan piped up and chided me good-naturedly, "So, do you still think you haven't learned anything of value?"

We all laughed, but I felt as if I had had a minor epiphany. Wow, I really *had* gotten enough to keep me from falling completely through the cracks these past tough ten years. And I realized something more. In that moment, there with my group, I realized for the first time that enough does not mean meager or insubstantial. It is not the opposite of abundance; rather, it is the very essence of it. Enough is about training our hearts, our minds and our spirits to embrace what we have in front of us, in the present, and trust that for right this minute, it is enough. It is this trust—that we will be given enough in every circumstance of life—that allows us to navigate, one trusting step at a time, from what may appear to be a rather spare present to a richly abundant future, however we may define that.

And, so, my friends, if someday you find yourself in Atlanta with your pineapples far away in Houston, fear not. I always keep a few extra on hand, and I would be happy to share them with you. It may not be a whole crate-load like you had counted on, but trust me when I say that it really will be enough.

Wishing you Godspeed and nothing but good bounces from here on out!

CPSIA information can be obtained at www.ICGtesting.com
Printed in the USA
LVOW08s0947291213

367280LV00001B/30/P